T0222811

Foundations of Popfly

Rapid Mashup Development

∎∎∎

Eric Griffin

Apress®

Foundations of Popfly: Rapid Mashup Development

Copyright © 2008 by Eric Griffin

ISBN-13 (pbk): 978-1-59059-951-8

ISBN-10 (pbk): 1-59059-951-9

ISBN-13 (electronic): 978-1-4302-0568-5

ISBN-10 (electronic): 1-4302-0568-7

Lead Editor: Ben Renow-Clarke
Technical Reviewer: Sarje Page
Editorial Board: Steve Anglin, Ewan Buckingham, Tony Campbell, Gary Cornell, Jonathan Gennick,
    Kevin Goff, Jonathan Hassell, Matthew Moodie, Joseph Ottinger, Jeffrey Pepper, Ben Renow-Clarke,
    Dominic Shakeshaft, Matt Wade, Tom Welsh
Project Manager: Kylie Johnston
Copy Editor: Heather Lang
Associate Production Director: Kari Brooks-Copony
Production Editor: Ellie Fountain
Compositor: Susan Glinert Stevens
Proofreader: Nancy Sixsmith
Indexer: Carol Burbo
Artist: Kinetic Publishing Services, LLC
Cover Designer: Kurt Krames
Manufacturing Director: Tom Debolski

Distributed to the book trade worldwide by Springer-Verlag New York, Inc., 233 Spring Street, 6th Floor, New York, NY 10013. Phone 1-800-SPRINGER, fax 201-348-4505, e-mail orders-ny@springer-sbm.com, or visit http://www.springeronline.com.

For information on translations, please contact Apress directly at 2855 Telegraph Avenue, Suite 600, Berkeley, CA 94705. Phone 510-549-5930, fax 510-549-5939, e-mail info@apress.com, or visit http://www.apress.com.

The source code for this book is available to readers at http://www.apress.com.

The book is dedicated to my wife, Susan, who is my source of unending support, love, and understanding.

Contents at a Glance

Contents

About the Author

ERIC GRIFFIN works as a Microsoft consultant. He is based in Atlanta and specializes in Microsoft Application Development technologies, tools, and platforms. This includes Visual Studio, SQL Server, ASP.NET, C#, Reporting Services, Office, SharePoint Server, and more.

About the Technical Reviewer

SARJE PAGE is a consultant with Qualesco Consulting Group, where he specializes in Microsoft technologies and relational database management systems. In the last ten years, he has designed, deployed, and optimized many data-oriented software applications while working as an information technology consultant for leading companies in the consumer products, construction, and insurance industries.

Acknowledgments

I would like to thank my technical reviewer, Sarje Page, for his comments during the writing of this book.

Introduction

When I heard that Microsoft was developing a mashup creation tool, I knew two things: one, that I wanted to get access to it as soon as possible, and two, that I wanted to write a book about it.

Mashups are all the rage. The explosion of public APIs by the who's who in the Web 2.0 world (Google, Yahoo, Microsoft, and so on) has caused a revolution in the way software is developed—mashups are the precursor to the way software will be developed in the future. Software as a service has long been on the horizon, and Web Services, in its many technological forms, is the enabler of cross-platform, cross-service integration that is at the heart of mashups.

But even as mashups emerged, the tools used to create them were familiar only to Web-savvy programmers and enthusiasts. For the larger, nontechnical audience, the tools were unapproachable and difficult to use.

Then Microsoft introduced Popfly—a tool for the nonprogrammer enthusiast who wants to quickly create new software.

Who This Book Is For

This book is for the nonprogrammer or enthusiast who wants to create new software fast. The tool enables users to take advantage of the heavy lifting already done by other programmers and the functionality supplied by public APIs in the form of Web Services from service providers like Microsoft, Yahoo, Google, and more.

How This Book Is Structured

This book consists of ten chapters. The first six chapters show you how to use the Popfly environment to create mashups, and the last four teach you to create components, called blocks, that can be used to create mashups within Popfly.

Chapter 1

Because mashups use technologies that are familiar to Web-savvy programmers in new and exciting ways, they are popping up everywhere—inspiring seasoned programmers and amateurs like. In this chapter, I introduce you to mashups and the rich world of creativity and freedom they offer. Mashups allow you to mix and match competing vendor APIs to create new, fun, and sometimes strange products and services.

Chapter 2

In this chapter, you see how Popfly hides the complex technologies needed to create mashups through the use of its simple tools, which require no coding. It also has an online community that fosters sharing, copying, and feedback.

Chapter 3

In Chapter 3, you create your first Popfly mashup. The mashup retrieves an RSS feed from a blog and displays it in a News Reader using blocks that you configure and connect in Popfly's block designer. You also add HTML to your mashup page.

Chapter 4

In this chapter, you create two more mashups: one using the Flickr photo service and PhotoSphere blocks and another using the Upcoming service (a Yahoo web site that provides dates of entertainment events) and Virtual Earth. You learn how to generate and manage API keys and how add custom code to modify a block. You also learn to retrieve information from the user and pass it on to blocks with the User Input block.

Chapter 5

In this chapter, you create your own web page using Popfly's Page Editor. You learn how to customize page styles and layouts and how to insert shared mashups onto web pages for the world to see.

Chapter 6

This chapter explains the four ways that Popfly supplies for you to share your mashups with external users: web pages, Windows Vista gadgets, Windows Live Spaces, and Facebook. You also learn how to e-mail your mashup.

Chapter 7

This chapter teaches you how blocks are defined (with XML) and executed (with JavaScript). You examine the RSS and News Reader blocks from previous examples to see how the block definitions and code are used together. You will learn about the Popfly Runtime Environment (PRE) and some of the helper functions it provides to make retrieving data from external sources easier.

Chapter 8

In this chapter, you examine the Popfly Block SDK. We'll look at the Popfly SDK test harness, which was created with .NET technology, and how to run it in a free tool from Microsoft called Visual Web Developer.

Chapter 9

In this chapter, you learn to use the rich functionality within Microsoft's Visual Web Developer to create blocks using the Popfly Block SDK. I'll explain how to amend a block's JavaScript file and block definition files in its editor. You also learn about Visual Web Developer's debugging capabilities and how to use the Block SDK schema files to help write and validate block definition files.

Chapter 10

This chapter teaches you to use Popfly's Block Creator to create or add your block to the Popfly environment for use in mashups. The Block Creator is not as rich as an integrated development environment like Visual Web Developer, but it has some basic code completion functionality to help you write your block code. You will also learn how to copy, or rip, code from other blocks to help you learn how it works or to give you a head start on your own blocks.

Prerequisites

Some knowledge of JavaScript and the technologies surrounding it, like AJAX and JSON, would be very helpful, as would knowledge of XML. No experience with Popfly is needed, and experience with software development kits (SDKs) and integrated development environments (IDEs) is not required but will be helpful.

Downloading the Code

You can find the Popfly Technorati Block created as a sample in this block from www.apress.com in the Downloads section of this book's home page. Please feel free to visit the Apress web site and download all the code there. You can also check for errata and find related titles from Apress.

Contacting the Author

You can reach Eric Griffin at his personal e-mail address at ebgriffin1968@hotmail.com.

CHAPTER 1

■ ■ ■

Introduction to Mashups

Mashups are inspiring a new generation of technology enthusiasts and programmers. Mashups enable experienced, web savvy programmers to integrate with the giants of the Web 2.0 space. As the name implies, mashups mix and "mash" the programming interfaces from different companies' products and services to create new products and services. Yahoo, Google, Amazon, eBay, and Microsoft have published *application programming interfaces* (APIs) based on web standards that allow you to utilize their complicated functionality without being a programming expert. Dozens more companies, big and small, have followed in the same way, creating a mashup explosion of API mixing and matching. New, sometimes strange, mashup creations pop up all the time.

In this chapter, I will explain what mashups are and give you a brief history of how mashups evolved and what technologies are used to create mashups. I will also give you a small sample of the dozens of products, services, and resources that are available to make mashups.

What Is a Mashup?

A mashup is the evolution of the way web applications are made: it allows a programmer to integrate products and services from competing companies like Microsoft, Google, Amazon, and Yahoo to create new, unique products and services, as illustrated in Figure 1-1.

These new products and services integrate APIs published by each company using web technologies that have evolved over the history of the web applications. We will look at these technologies in more detail later on in the chapter.

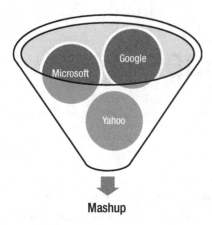

Figure 1-1. *Mashups can be created using APIs from competing companies.*

A Brief History of Mashups

It will be difficult to detail the history of mashups without understanding the broader context of the history of the Web and how it has spurred the emergence of mashups.

Have you heard of Web 2.0? If you haven't, don't worry; this will be the first of many encounters with this phrase. Web 2.0 was coined in 2001 by Tim O'Reilly after the dot com crash. From a technical perspective, the word "Web" refers to the products, services, and business models that are created using the Internet as a platform. This is contrary to the PC or desktop computers being used as a platform. The "2.0" implies an upgrade from 1.0 products, services, and business models and the previous generation of technologies used to create those products and services. The new generation of technologies in Web 2.0 make web sites function and respond dynamically, like desktop applications.

Web 1.0 companies built products and services that would lock their customers in. They accomplished this by controlling the customers' data.

Note When I talk about customer data, I am referring to anything that the customer perceives as valuable. It doesn't have to be important to another customer. It is personal data but not necessarily sensitive like a Social Security number or address. And customers don't have to own the data. Examples of customers' data could be the weather forecasts in their city, a query on a search engine to find a consumer review web site because they want to buy a camera, a gallery of photos they want to share with family, or a subscription to a financial feed that tracks their favorite stocks. All of the examples show how data can be important to an individual, and that is the key to its value.

Let's look at the example of portals offered by vendors Netscape and Yahoo back in 1997. Customers logged in (using a vender-specific ID, of course) and customized his portals to access news, weather, and sports to their liking. It saved this information for them and updated it regularly. However, the news, sports, and weather were from sources offered only by that portal alone or by the portal vendor (e.g., you only had access to Yahoo News, Yahoo Sports, and so on). And it was likely the source of data had to pay to be available to the customer, and it might be available exclusively. In this model, by controlling the data, the portal vendors would create barriers to entry by centralizing and controlling data that was valuable to the customer. To get to data, customers had to go to that vendor's products and services.

In addition to being controlled, data was isolated without the ability to be integrated with other data from other sources. There was no easy way for the customer to tie two different bits of logically groupable data in a meaningful way. For example, there was no way to merge information about an event at a local park with the weather forecast or a directory of Italian restaurants with a map of your area.

Web 1.0 API technologies were proprietary and often built with standards that were PC based and not web friendly—plug-ins, C interfaces and dynamic link libraries (DLLs). These APIs, frequently packaged in software development kits (SDKs), were about getting the programmer immersed and invested in mastering the vendor's APIs. There were developer programs and conferences touting one vendor API over another.

Web 2.0 represents how business models built on the Internet evolved from Web 1.0. After the dot com bomb in 2001, a small wave of companies emerged with a different perspective on how to leverage the Internet. That leverage came from opening up the customer data their products and services controlled. Using web standards that were common and widely adopted across traditional competitors, a new value proposition was created. This value proposition supercharged start-ups like Google, Amazon, and eBay and revitalized established Internet players like Microsoft and Yahoo.

Portals in Web 2.0 put customers in charge of their data. Let's return to the example of portals and now move forward to 2008: myYahoo, Microsoft Live, and iGoogle not only enable the customer to completely control what data they see and what source it comes from, but where on the page and how often it is displayed. Each bit of data, contained in what is called a portlet, is customizable to further give customers control over their data. If you like Google's portal but love Yahoo Sports and MSNBC News, you can get access to them inside Google's portal.

Creating new content for modern portals is based on open standards. Gone are the proprietary SDKs that are bound to vendor platform products and services. Now, a programmer can leverage the same fundamental technical knowledge to develop for Google, Yahoo, or Microsoft, as all the APIs use the same technologies, like HTML, CSS, and JavaScript.

Web 2.0 technologies play a big part in the advancement of portals. The fact is that modern portals are mashups. Mashups enable the retrieval and control of data by using the open APIs provided by service providers. In the next section, we will detail the technologies important to mashup development.

Understanding Mashup Technology

As with all technologies, mashup technologies evolved over time. Figure 1-2 shows the progression of technologies that emerged and serve as a foundation for mashup development.

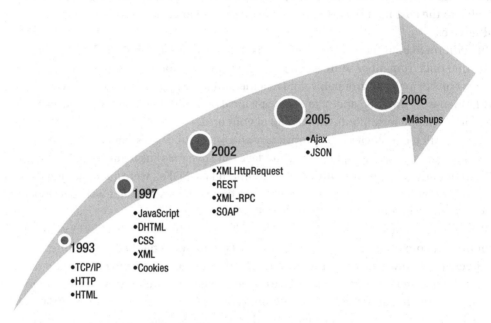

Figure 1-2. *Mashup technology timeline*

The most important thing to remember is not when a particular technology was created but when it became relevant to the overall community. One key factor is wide vendor adoption.

JavaScript would not be as important today if it had not been adopted by Microsoft and Netscape in their browsers. Netscape created JavaScript (originally called LiveScript) in 1995 in its browser Netscape Navigator. It wasn't until late 1996 that Microsoft shipped JScript (its own implementation of JavaScript) in its browser Internet Explorer. JavaScript became a de facto standard because it was used by virtually 100 percent of the market's browsers. Any newcomers in the browser arena had to implement JavaScript to be considered a viable alternative browser.

JSON was introduced as a JavaScript-based data format in 1999. It took over seven years to become relevant to the web development community. But as the web development community realized the need for a simple lightweight way to transfer data besides XML, JSON was rediscovered.

Before each of these technologies is explained, it is important to further categorize them into the roles they play in mashup development, which is done in Figure 1-3.

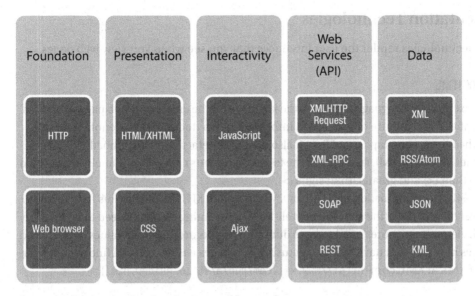

Figure 1-3. *Categorized technologies used by mashups*

Foundation Technologies

You can't build a house without a foundation. The same statement holds true for creating mashups. There are two technologies that provide the foundation for all the others: HTTP and the web browser. There are dozens of books written on each of these technologies, and they are fairly well known in general, so I won't go into detail now. But it is always important to know how things work and interrelate, so I will give a broad overview here.

HTTP

Hypertext Transfer Protocol (HTTP) is the protocol that enables us to navigate the Web. HTTP is a request/response protocol among clients and servers. An HTTP client initiates a request by establishing a TCP connection to a particular port on a remote host. An HTTP server listening on that port waits for the client to send it a request for a web page and then sends the client the web page it requests, provided the client has the relevant permissions to access that page.

Web Browser

The delivery platform for mashups and all other web-based applications and sites is the web browser. A web browser is a software application that enables a user to display and interact with text, images, and other information. It hosts the technologies within the presentation, interactivity, web services, and data layers. The web browser uses HTTP to request web pages and data from remote servers. There are many browsers available today: Internet Explorer, Firefox, Opera, Safari, Camino (specifically on Mac OS), and Konqueror (specifically on Linux); there are even text-only browsers such as Lynx.

Presentation Technologies

These technologies render the user interfaces that you see when you view web pages.

HTML/XHTML

Hypertext Markup Language (HTML) is the language for the creation of web page structures. It describes the structure of text-based information in a document by denoting certain text as headings, paragraphs, and lists. It also denotes interactive forms, embedded images, and other objects. HTML is written in the form of elements called *tags*—labels surrounded by less-than (<) and greater-than signs (>).

XHTML is a reformulation of HTML in XML, therefore XHTML documents have to follow the strict rules of XML (they have to be well-formed, meaning elements need to be properly closed, element attributes need to have quotation marks around their values, etc.). It also provides new tags that have made structuring web pages easier. You can find a great overview of XML at XML.com (`http://www.xml.com/pub/a/98/10/guide0.html`).

CSS

Cascading Style Sheets (CSS) is a language used to describe the presentation of a document written in a markup language. It is used to style web pages written in HTML and XHTML by defining rules that specify how markup should be styled and positioned.

Interactivity Technologies

The interactive technologies are used to create custom dynamic behavior like showing or hiding content, dragging and dropping of content, and animations. Without interactivity in web pages, you are left with bland, static uninspired functionality that doesn't provide the same robust interaction that a desktop application provides.

JavaScript

JavaScript is a scripting language used in web browsers to provide interactivity to web pages. It is compliant with a script standard called ECMAScript. JavaScript is the Mozilla Foundation's (originally created by Netscape Communications Corporation) implementation of the ECMAScript standard.

JavaScript was influenced by many languages and was designed to have a similar look to Java but be easier for nonprogrammers to work with. Contrary to its name, JavaScript is unrelated to the Java programming language. The language was renamed from LiveScript in a comarketing deal between Netscape and Sun in exchange for Netscape bundling Sun's Java runtime with its browser, which was dominant at the time.

I could spend the entire book focusing on JavaScript. Knowledge of JavaScript is not required to create basic mashups with Popfly, but it is required when you want to extend

Popfly's functionality with Popfly Blocks. There are dozens of books that can give you a deeper insight into it. I have listed some here:

- *Beginning JavaScript with DOM Scripting and Ajax: From Novice to Professional* by Christian Heilmann (Apress, 2006)

- *Practical JavaScript, DOM Scripting, and Ajax Projects* by Frank Zammetti (Apress, 2007)

- *Pro JavaScript Techniques* by John Resig (Apress, 2006)

Ajax

Ajax is a JavaScript development technique that is so important to Web 2.0 development that it should be considered a separate technology. The name is an acronym standing for Asynchronous JavaScript and XML. It is a culmination of the trend in developing web applications that respond like desktop applications.

Ajax is asynchronous in that loading does not interfere with normal page loading and does not require that the entire web page be reloaded each time the user requests a change. For example, if you update the quantities in a shopping cart, the site could use Ajax to instantly display the new price and shipping total without having to waste time reloading the entire page again. Ajax increases a web page's interactivity, speed, functionality, and usability. JavaScript is the programming language Ajax function calls are made in. Data retrieved using the technique is commonly formatted using XML and JSON.

Web Service Technologies: Application Programming Interfaces

When vendors want to create APIs for their products and services on the Web, web services are the means to do it. There are many options for vendors to use. Mashups use web service technologies to access a vendor's product functionality.

XMLHttpRequest

Before we go into the various types of web services, it is important to call out the most important component of the emergence of web services as a way to create web APIs—XMLHttpRequest.

XMLHttpRequest is not a web service technology but an API that is available in JavaScript, to send data to and from a web server using HTTP, by establishing an independent communication channel between a web page's client side and server side.

The data returned from XMLHttpRequest calls are often provided by back-end databases. Besides XML, XMLHttpRequest can be used to fetch data in other formats such as HTML, JSON, or plain text.

XMLHttpRequest is an important part of the Ajax web development technique, and it is used by many web sites to implement responsive and dynamic web applications.

XML-RPC

XML-RPC is a remote procedure call protocol that uses XML to encode its calls and HTTP as a transport mechanism.

SOAP

Simple Object Access Protocol or Service Oriented Architecture Protocol (SOAP) is a protocol for exchanging XML-based messages over computer networks, normally using HTTP/HTTPS. SOAP forms the foundation layer of many web services, providing a basic messaging framework those more abstract layers can build on.

REST

Representational State Transfer (REST) is a style of web service that uses HTTP Universal Resource Locators (URLs) for function calls. When you navigate to a web page, you are using a form of REST. For example, the URL from this Yahoo search from a web browser is a REST call: http://search.yahoo.com/search?p=ajax&fr=yfp-t-501&toggle=1&cop=mss&ei=UTF-8. In this example the URL points to the search home URL at search.yahoo.com/search and sends parameters of the search after the question mark (?) separated by the ampersand sign (&).

Data Technologies

Everything begins and ends with data. The Internet is a global tool to publish, organize, and share data. With that in mind, it is important to understand the formats commonly used in mashups to send, receive, and store data. Remember, the content of data can be endless. It can contain search results, links, photos, news, video, geographic locations, and audio. The list of content that can be formatted and delivered grows all the time.

XML

To say that XML is an important part of how data is used in mashups is an understatement. XML seems to be the foundation for everything these days. XML is not the data itself but a way to represent the data using elements to provide structure, in the same way HTML does. The difference between HTML and XML is that with XML you can create your own custom elements to represent data in any way you want, whereas HTML is just for marking up web pages. XML's primary purpose is to facilitate the sharing of data across different information systems, particularly via the Internet.

RSS/Atom

Really Simple Syndication (RSS) is one of the key technologies that have freed customer and vendor data. RSS is a web-feed format used to publish frequently updated content such as blog entries, news headlines, or podcasts. An RSS document, which is called a feed, web feed, or channel, contains either a summary of content from an associated web site or the full text. Users can use RSS readers on the Web or on the desktop to subscribe to the feed to receive any updates. Based on XML and transported on HTTP, RSS has become a standard for publishing text, video, and audio.

The name Atom applies to a pair of related standards. The Atom Syndication Format is an XML language used for web feeds, while the Atom Publishing Protocol (APP for short) is a simple HTTP-based protocol for creating and updating Web resources.

JSON

JavaScript Object Notation (JSON) is a lightweight computer data interchange format. It is a text-based, human-readable format for representing objects and other data structures and is mainly used to transmit such structured data over a network connection (in a process called serialization).

JSON finds its main application in Ajax web application programming, as a simple alternative to using XML for asynchronously transmitting structured information between client and server.

KML

Keyhole Markup Language (KML) is an XML-based language for managing the display of three-dimensional geospatial data in the mapping web applications like Google Maps and Microsoft Virtual Earth.

Mashup Architecture

Now that we've gone through most of the dizzying array of technologies used to create mashups, it's important to know how all of them interrelate—how they fit together in an architecture. From an architectural perspective, the categories of mashup technologies can be seen as layers, as shown in Figure 1-4. A layer is a logical representation of where these technologies reside and how they are separated within a mashup.

As of this writing, mashups are primarily being hosted in web browsers. Mashups are also being hosted by operating systems like Windows Vista, in the form of Windows Sidebar Gadgets, and Mac OSX, as dashboard widgets. It is safe to assume that mashups in the future will be hosted in environments that closely emulate the web browser. Figure 1-4 details a generic mashup architecture.

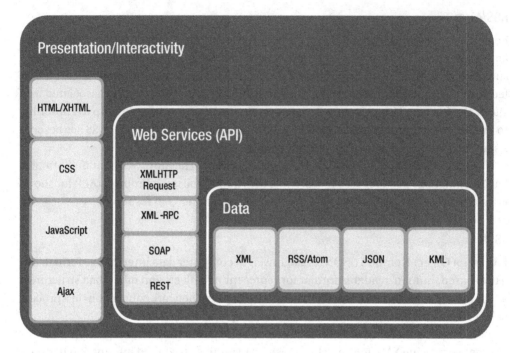

Figure 1-4. *Mashup architecture layers*

The presentation and interactivity layer is the user interface of the mashup. HTML, styled with CSS, displays the mashup interface to the user. JavaScript, with Ajax techniques, enhances the user's experience by making the mashup more responsive and desktop-application like. JavaScript also receives the user's input and, if necessary, initiates requests to the web services APIs used by the mashup.

For example, in a book search web application, users could search for a book they want to buy by entering the book's ISBN into the interface. Regardless if we're talking about XML-RPC, SOAP, or REST web services, XMLHTTPRequest is used to send the book's ISBN using XML or JSON to the server.

The book data (e.g., price, author, abstract and so on) stored on the server is retrieved from a database of books and formatted (usually in XML, but increasingly in JSON) before it is returned to the presentation and interactivity layer.

Once returned, JavaScript is used display the book's title, author, and cover image using HTML with CSS.

Examples of Mashups

As of late 2007, Programmable Web has over 2,000 mashups listed. That's way too many to list here, so I picked out some representative mashups that have caught my eye and use some of the mashup APIs we'll be talking about in this book.

AP News + Google Maps

AP News + Google Maps (`http://www.81nassau.com/apnews`) is a very interesting site that is a great example of how mashups use data and APIs from different sources to create a new product (see Figure 1-5). This site displays the Associated Press U.S. National, Sports, Business and Technology, and Strange news stories on top of Google Maps.

It retrieves a published RSS feed from the Associated Press web site and translates (using the Yahoo Geo-encoding REST API) the city and state from each story into a latitude and longitude point. Google Maps is used to plot the points on a map.

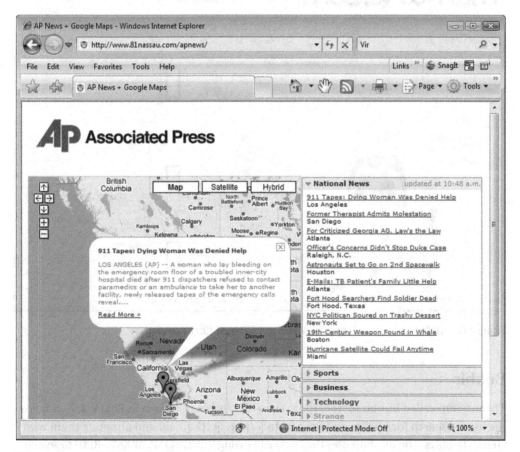

Figure 1-5. *API News + Google Maps: mashup of the Associated Press RSS feed, Yahoo Geo-encoding, and Google Maps*

Markovic.com

Markovic.com (`http://www.markovic.com/markovic.com/ebay/search-virtual-earth.php`) is a mashup that displays items for sale on eBay and the seller's location using Microsoft Virtual Earth; see Figure 1-6. The mashup communicates (using SOAP and REST) with the eBay API to enable customers to search for items they are interested in buying. A list is returned in XML format that enables the developer to plot the location of the seller and display it using the Virtual Earth API.

Figure 1-6. *Markovic.com: mashup of Microsoft Virtual Earth and eBay APIs*

Bubblr

The mashup called Bubblr (`http://pimpampum.net/bubblr`), shown in Figure 1-7, enables the user to search for photos on Flickr (`http://www.flickr.com`) and annotate them with speech bubbles. The mashup uses the Flickr API (using REST, SOAP, or XML-RPC) to search for tagged photos (e.g., photos labeled as "baby", "party", or "beach") or retrieve photos using the customer's Flickr user ID. Once users find photos they are interested in, they can annotate the picture with dialog balloons.

Figure 1-7. *Bubblr: mashup using the Flickr API and custom picture editing*

The examples I have shown here are a very small representative sampling of the variety of mashups. The combinations of APIs are endless.

Mashup Resources on the Web

In the following sections, I've listed some of the most useful mashup resources that exist on the Web. You should take the time to check them out!

Web Sites

Many web sites and blogs talk about mashups; I will recommend the best ones I have found.

Programmable Web

The best source of new and existing vendor APIs and the mashups using them is Programmable Web (`http://www.programmableweb.com`). New mashups and vendor APIs are added daily. I would start here if you want to see what's going on in the world of mashups.

TechCrunch

TechCrunch (`http://www.techcrunch.com`) is a weblog that reports news and announcements from startups and companies that are considered a part of Web 2.0. Startups with business models that include mashup technology in their products and services are often covered.

Mashable

Social networking web sites use mashup technology to give their users more control over creating, mixing, and sharing their data with a community of users. Mashable (`http://www.mashable.com`) covers the social networking space and has frequent news about MySpace, Facebook, Friendster, and other social networking sites.

Mashup Web Service APIs

There seem to be new mashup web service APIs popping up all the time. Programmable Web lists over 400 APIs and counting. The explosion of APIs is directly related to how many new Web 2.0 startups come to market. As stated previously, if you are creating a Web 2.0 product or service, there is no way around *not* creating mashable APIs for it. Programmable Web and the other web sites are the best source for up-to-the-minute mashup APIs being created; I won't list all of them here.

However, the APIs from companies like Google, Microsoft, Amazon, Yahoo, and eBay have been around for a while and are considered the best places to start. When you look across the APIs offered by these companies, you begin to see how these APIs are grouped. Figure 1-8 shows how the APIs are categorized into Mapping, Photo, Search, Video, and e-Commerce.

Over time, the categories and lists of APIs is sure to grow as the Internet consumes more valuable data that customers use.

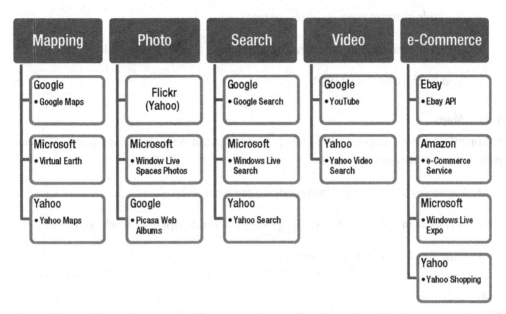

Figure 1-8. *APIs from Google, Microsoft, Yahoo, Amazon, and eBay categories by function*

Mapping

Geographic coordinates (locations) can be displayed (in aerial or roadmap views) in remarkable detail. Integrating the display data with location information about business, roads, and landmarks allows directions from point to point to be determined.

Mapping is the first and most popular mashup API that is widely adopted and used by the programming community. Google Maps, which in 2002 was the first mapping API, is by far the most often used.

Microsoft Virtual Earth

Microsoft's online mapping platform is available to web developers as well as Live Search customers. Here are the details on Virtual Earth:

- *Available at*: http://dev.live.com/virtualearth/

- *API used*: JavaScript interaction with embedded JavaScript control

- *Data format*: XML

Google Maps

You can embed maps in your own web pages using the Google Maps JavaScript API and included geocoding service:

- *Available at*: http://www.google.com/apis/maps/

- *API used*: JavaScript interaction with embedded JavaScript control

- *Data formats*: XML and JSON

Yahoo Maps

Yahoo offers several mapping APIs that can integrate a store locator, view highway traffic patterns, or create custom routes:

- *Available at*: http://developer.yahoo.com/maps/

- *APIs used*: JavaScript with JavaScript Control, JavaScript with Flash, and REST

- *Data formats*: XML, HTML, and text

Photo

Photo sharing among friends and family is very popular. It's an important piece of data that customers can't find enough ways to tag, categorize, comment, and share with the world.

Yahoo's Flickr

Flickr is the world's most popular photo sharing service:

- *Available at*: http://www.flickr.com/services/

- *APIs used*: REST, SOAP, and XML-RPC

- *Data formats*: XML and JSON

Microsoft Windows Live Photos

If you or your site visitors have a Windows Live Spaces account, you can use the Windows Live Spaces control with client-side JavaScript to let visitors use their Windows Live Spaces photos with your web site. Windows Live Spaces control is a bit complicated on the inside, but on the outside, you only have to create a `spacescontrol` element and event handlers to receive the selected photo data:

- *Available at*: http://dev.live.com/spacescontrol/api.aspx

- *API used*: JavaScript interacting with a JavaScript control

- *Data format*: None

Google Picasa Web Album

If you use Google's Picasa Web Album, you can use its web API to retrieve a list of photos, tags, comments, or user albums:

- *Available at*: http://code.google.com/apis/picasaweb/overview.html

- *API used*: REST

- *Data formats*: RSS and Atom

Search

Searching is at the heart of the Internet. Without it, you wouldn't be able to navigate the billions of web pages on the Web.

Google Search

Google has an API that allows you to search in your web pages with JavaScript. A search box can be embedded in your pages, and you can display the search results it returns:

- *Available at*: http://code.google.com/

- *API used*: SOAP

- *Data format*: XML

Windows Live Search

This API allows developers to programmatically submit queries and retrieve results from the Windows Live search engine:

- *Available at*: http://dev.live.com/livesearch/

- *API used*: SOAP

- *Data format*: XML

Yahoo Search

There are four search types within the Yahoo Search service:

- *Contextual Web Search*: Finds related sites based on keywords

- *Related Suggestion*: Returns suggested queries.

- *Spelling Suggestion*: Spellchecks text that you send it

- *Web Search*: Searches web sites

Here are the details on the Yahoo Search service:

- *Available at*: http://developer.yahoo.com/search/

- *API used*: REST

- *Data format*: XML

Video

With consumer video recording technology reaching millions, more and users are sharing, categorizing, and commenting on videos uploaded to online services, just like they do with photos.

Google's YouTube

YouTube is a vast repository of videos about every imaginable topic. You can use YouTube's API to integrate online videos into your web site:

- *Available at*: http://www.youtube.com/dev

Yahoo Video Search

The Video Search service allows you to search the Internet for video clips:

- *Available at*: http://developer.yahoo.com/search/video/V1/videoSearch.html

- *API used*: REST

- *Data format*: XML

E-commerce

The monetization of the Internet first started with your basic banner ad at the top of web pages. Buying merchandize online was unheard of and thought to be unsafe. Today, online buying is in the billions of dollars annually, with companies like Amazon and eBay leading the way.

Note that APIs relating to search advertising are not listed here.

eBay API

By joining the eBay Developers Program, you can build applications using eBay web services. It provides functionality for shopping, searching, and monitoring sales of your online shop:

- *Available at*: http://developer.ebay.com/

- *APIs used*: SOAP and REST

- *Data format*: XML

Amazon E-Commerce Services

Amazon's E-Commerce Services enables developers, web site owners, and merchants to access product data and e-commerce functionality:

- *Available at*: http://www.amazon.com/gp/browse.html/ref=sc_fe_l_2/
  103-1644811-9832630?%5Fencoding=UTF8&node=12738641&no=3435361

- *APIs used*: SOAP and REST

- *Data format*: XML

Microsoft Windows Live Expo

Windows Live Expo, with its vast list of real estate, automobiles, jobs, and online merchandise can be accessed via a set of web services called Expo API:

- *Available at*: http://dev.live.com/expo/

- *APIs used*: SOAP and REST.

- *Data formats*: XML

Yahoo Shopping

You can display user reviews, search, and do comparison shopping using the Yahoo Shopping API:

- *Available at*: http://developer.yahoo.com/shopping/

- *APIs used*: SOAP and REST

- *Data formats*: XML

Summary

The Internet has evolved from what was called Web 1.0 to Web 2.0. Web 1.0 business models locked the customer into products and services by controlling the customer's data. In Web 2.0, business models unlocked customer's data by publishing application programming interfaces (APIs) using open technology standards that anyone can use.

Mashups offer a rich world of creativity and freedom; they mix and match competing vendor APIs to create new, fun, and sometimes strange products and services. Because mashups use technologies that are familiar to web savvy programmers, mashups are popping up everywhere inspiring programmers and enthusiasts.

In the next chapter, you will see how Microsoft's Popfly is the next generation of mashup technology that will enable a wider audience of nonprogrammers to enter the mashup frenzy.

CHAPTER 2

■ ■ ■

Enter Popfly

In Chapter 1, we explored the world of mashups, the new way to build web sites and gadgets using dozens of technologies that have evolved with the Web.

Because of the number of technologies used to create mashups, would-be mashup creators are required to have a significant amount of programming experience. Many have no intention of becoming professional programmers, and this makes mashup development unapproachable for the average person.

In May of 2007, Microsoft introduced Popfly (http://www.popfly.com). Figure 2-1 shows the home page. The stated goal was to enable nonprofessional programmers to create mashups without having to write a line of code.

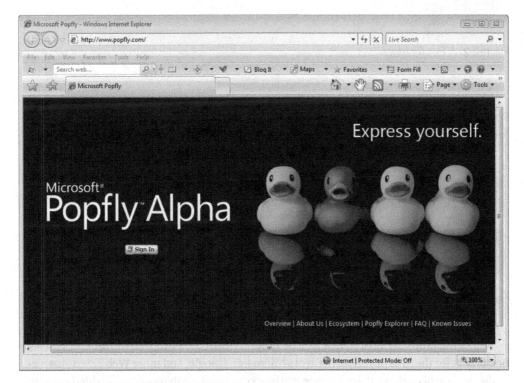

Figure 2-1. *Microsoft Popfly home page*

In this chapter I will give you an overview of the Popfly environment. You will learn about where mashups are created and show you some examples. We will also get you started with a Popfly account and profile so you can start participating in the online community

What Is Popfly?

Popfly is also an online community that enables its members the ability to rate, share, mix and remix mashups with other community members. Those users who are willing to learn some XML and JavaScript can extend Popfly by creating their own Popfly blocks.

Popfly makes mashup development easier by not requiring you to have knowledge of the complex technologies that underpin mashups. This is accomplished with visual metaphors (i.e., blocks) that can be dragged, dropped, configured, and linked together. Figure 2-2 shows a Popfly block. Popfly blocks, which we will discuss in greater detail in Chapter 3, are the building blocks (no pun intended) for mashup creation in Popfly.

Figure 2-2. *A Popfly block*

Figure 2-3 shows the technologies discussed in Chapter 1 that are encompassed within Popfly blocks: presentation, interactivity, web services, and data. Some blocks contain all four technologies.

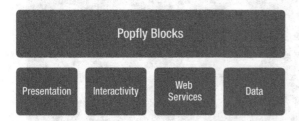

Figure 2-3. *Popfly includes mashup creation technologies.*

Popfly mashups are hosted in a web browser. Within the Popfly environment, you will find blocks for the APIs of Yahoo, Amazon, Microsoft, Google, and more Web 2.0 companies. At the time of this writing, there are over 200 blocks in Popfly with more being added each day.

Some examples of blocks are listed in the following sections.

Presentation and Interactivity Blocks

Presentation and interactivity blocks enable the user, via a user interface, to have direct control over the mashup:

- *Virtual Earth*: This presentation block will display Virtual Earth maps that you can further annotate with information, such as the bowling alleys in your city.

- *News Reader*: This presentation block displays a simple user interface for RSS feeds. You could connect it to the RSS block to display the latest news.

- *Photo Sphere, Photo Tiles, and PhotoFlip*: These blocks all display images, in different visual formats, from sources like Flickr and Windows Live Spaces.

- *SoapBox*: This block enables you to search for videos on MSN Soapbox (`http://soapbox.msn.com`) and displays a preview list of found videos you can select.

- *Stock Quotes*: This block displays a chart for a specified stock.

Web Services and Data Blocks

Web services are application programming interfaces (APIs) built on Internet standards that enable access to a service provider's data. Here are a few handy web services and data blocks:

- *Flickr*: If you have a Flickr account, you can configure this block to communicate with the Flickr web services to return specific images, such as a family picture from your summer vacation

- *RSS*: This data block will load an RSS feed from a remote source. This could be from a blog or a news source like CNN news.

- *Facebook*: Facebook, one of the leading online social networks, has APIs that are captured in this block. It enables you to share your mashup creations with other Facebook users.

- *Live Search*: This block connects to the Windows Live Web web services to search for images, videos, and web sites.

- *Yahoo Search*: If you prefer Yahoo, this block communicates with Yahoo's web services for its search engine.

Before I go into detail about how to use blocks to create mashups, I will go over the Popfly environment.

The Popfly Environment

The Popfly environment is where you create, share, and mix your mashups. It has four areas, or *spaces*:

- *Mashup Creator*: Create Stuff ➤ Mashup

- *Block Creator:* Create Stuff ➤ Web Page

- *Web Page Creator*: Create Stuff ➤ Block

- *Online community*: Create Stuff ➤ Popfly Explorer

Mashup Creator

This is the area within Popfly where blocks are used to create mashups. The interactive design surface is used to configure and link blocks.

The interactive design surface allows you to drag and drop blocks and connect them together to build your mashup without writing code. Connecting web services is as easy as drawing a line between two blocks. Figure 2-4 shows a Live Contacts block and a Facebook block connecting to a Virtual Earth block. Blocks available in Popfly are listed in the Blocks window. You can search for blocks by name by typing keywords into the search box at the top of the window.

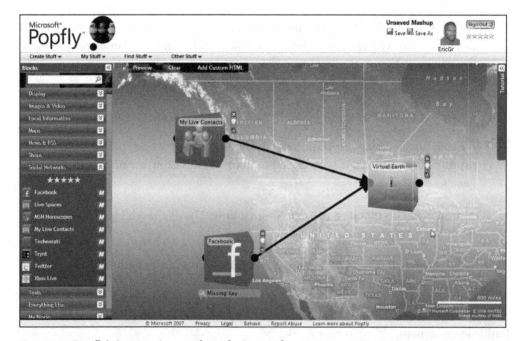

Figure 2-4. *Popfly's interactive mashup design surface*

Block Creator

This area is where you create custom Popfly blocks. You can search and copy or rip code from existing blocks to give you a head start on your block. Figure 2-5 shows the Block Creator. I will cover more on block creation in Chapter 7.

Figure 2-5. *Block Creator*

Web Page Creator

The Web Page Creator is a WYSIWYG HTML editor within the browser. You can create, publish, and host web pages in which to present your mashups to the world all within Popfly.

Figure 2-6 shows you the Web Page Creator. The Page Editor does not require you to know HTML. All of the text, layout, and style features are available via menus. I will go into further detail about the Web Page Creator in Chapter 5.

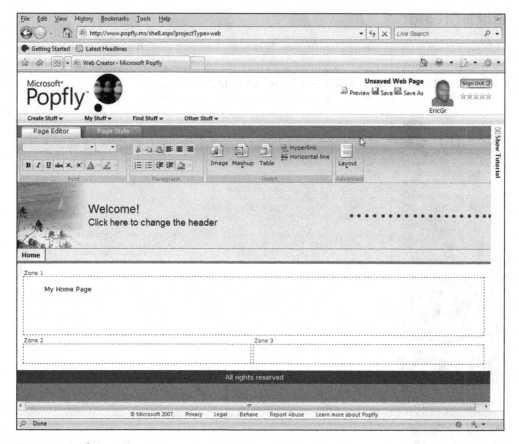

Figure 2-6. *Web Page Creator*

Popfly Explorer

Popfly Explorer is a Microsoft Visual Studio 2005 add-in that enables you create, modify, and share Visual Studio solutions from your Popfly space. Visual Studio is a programming environment with tools and technologies for professional programmers.

Online Community

Popfly is also an online community of creators where you can host, share, rate, comment, and even remix mashups from other Popfly users. The information displayed in the online community is built from the user profile pages (see Figure 2-7).

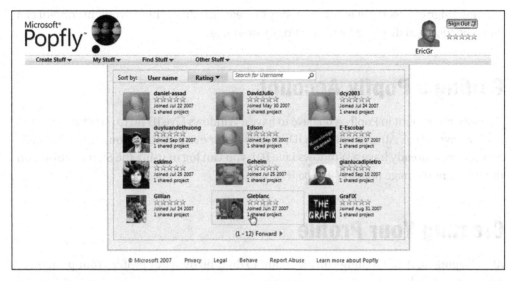

Figure 2-7. *Popfly users*

By clicking Share on your Projects page, your Popfly application will be hosted on Popfly and made available for anyone to use. You can also generate a set of codes you can use to insert your application on any site that supports the HTML `IFRAME` tag as well as being able to publish to any MetaWeblog API blog.

■**Note** `IFRAME` is an HTML tag that is used to embed web pages within another web page.

The MetaWeblog API is a web service used by blogging platforms like MovableType and WordPress. Blog hosting web sites like TypePad and Windows Live Spaces use it to enable their users to create blog posts from remote or desktop clients.

How Do Silverlight and Popfly Relate?

Silverlight is a new technology introduced by Microsoft in April 2007. It is a plug-in for web browsers that displays dynamic streaming content like video, audio, and images. User interfaces can be created in Silverlight to provide a desktop application experience. Popfly's environment is created in Silverlight. You need to install Silverlight before you can use Popfly. Instructions for installation are on Silverlight's home page (http://www.silverlight.net).

Knowledge of Silverlight is not necessary to create mashups, but Silverlight content can be embedded and displayed within a Popfly mashups.

Getting a Popfly Account

To create an account in Popfly, you have to have a Windows Live ID (`http://get.live.com/getlive/overview`). After creating an ID, or using your existing ID (if you have a Hotmail account, you already have a Windows Live ID), you can log in using the Sign In button on the Popfly home page (`http://www.popfly.com`).

Creating Your Profile

After logging in, the first thing you may want to do is fill out your profile. Your profile is your way to tell the community who you are.

You can access your profile by clicking My Stuff ➤ Edit My Stuff from the main menu located near your user ID (see Figure 2-8).

Figure 2-8. *Main Menu*

In the My Profile page, shown in Figure 2-9, you can fill in your name and other information including a picture of yourself representing you as an avatar. You can also, if you have a blog, enter your RSS feed information into your profile, so others can read entries from your blog.

After you have edited your profile, click Submit Changes to save the changes or Cancel if you want to discard your updates.

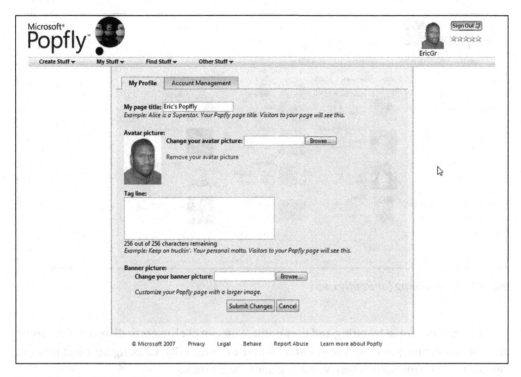

Figure 2-9. *The My Profile page*

Finding Users

You can find other users in the community by selecting Find Stuff ➤ Search People (see Figure 2-10).

Figure 2-10. *The Find Stuff menu*

The user community screen appears (see Figure 2-11), where you can see various users. As you type in the search box, the list of matching found users is updated.

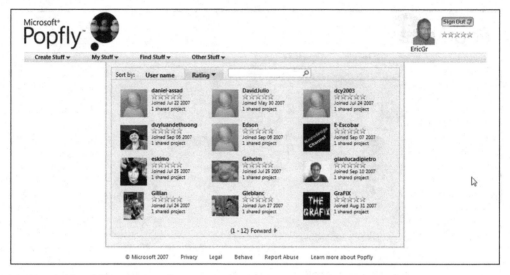

Figure 2-11. *Searching for Popfly users*

Users can be sorted by rating and user name. You can click users to display their Popfly friends and the projects they have shared with the community. Clicking a project name takes you to the mashup, where you can explore and rate it.

Getting Help

You can get help in Popfly by clicking Other Stuff ➤ Forums. It will take you to the Microsoft forum for Popfly at `http://forums.microsoft.com/MSDN/default.aspx?ForumGroupID=434&SiteID=1`.

Popfly also has a built-in help available by clicking Other Stuff ➤ Help.

Popfly Examples

I browsed through the hundreds of mashups shared by the Popfly community and found many interesting and strange ones; some were rated high by the community, some low. I picked out three as examples to show you.

Upcoming Music Events with Forecast

This mashup looks up music concerts from Yahoo's Upcoming block (`http://upcoming.yahoo.com/`) and combines it with weather forecasts from WeatherBug (http://weather.weatherbug.com/) for each concert's location. It also displays the concert locations in a Virtual Earth block (see Figure 2-12).

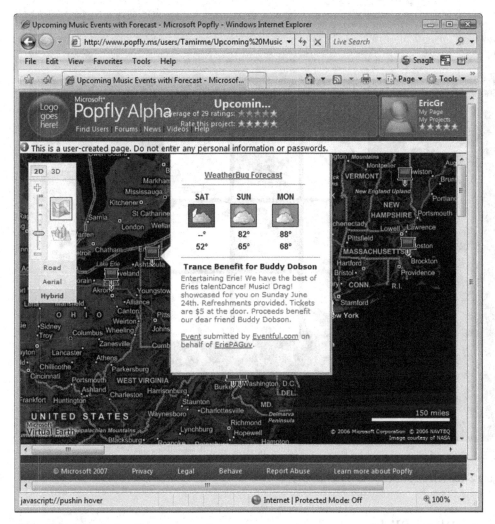

Figure 2-12. *Upcoming Concerts mashup*

My Facebook Friends

This mashup combines a Photo display block with the creator's Facebook account via the Facebook block. Pictures from the user's Facebook friends list are displayed, and clicking a picture takes you to that user's Facebook site.

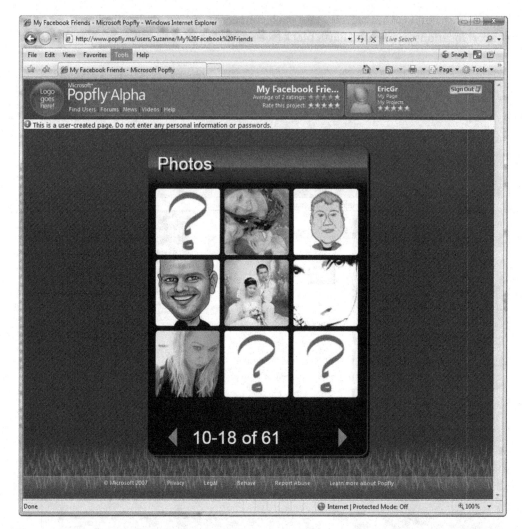

Figure 2-13. *The My Facebook Friends block*

spacesPhotoSlide

The spacesPhotoSlide mashup shows a user's family photos taken during a trip to Italy that have been uploaded to a Windows Live Spaces account. The pictures are displayed using a Photo display block that is fed by the Spaces photo block. Dynamic animation flips backward and forward through the pictures as if you were holding them in your hand (see Figure 2-14).

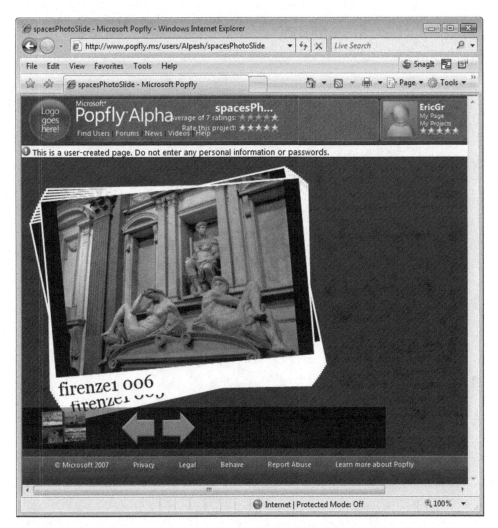

Figure 2-14. *A Mashup showing a family trip photos from Windows Live Spaces*

Summary

Microsoft Popfly was introduced in May 2007 as a way to encourage nonprogrammers to get into creating mashups. As you've seen, Popfly hides the complex technologies needed to create mashups through the use of its simple tools that require no coding. It also has an online community that fosters sharing, copying, and feedback.

In the next chapter you will learn the skills you can use to create your first mashup.

CHAPTER 3

■■■

Creating Your First Mashup

In Chapter 2, you learned that Microsoft Popfly is not only a tool for creating mashups, but an online community where users can share, mix, and rate their creations. In this chapter, you will create your first mashup. Along the way, you will learn the skills you can use to create your own mashups.

Before you can begin, you need to have a Popfly account. The instructions for creating your account are detailed in Chapter 2. Once you have your account, log in, and select My Stuff ➤ Projects. Click Create Stuff ➤ Mashup. This opens up the mashup design surface (see Figure 3-1).

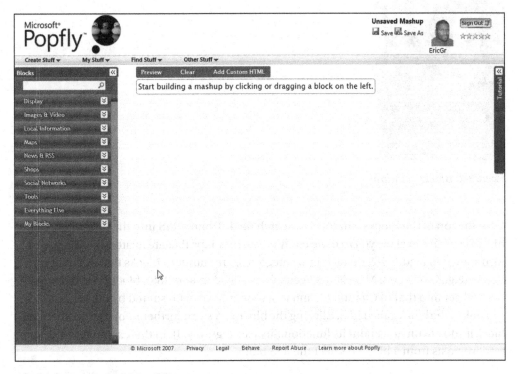

Figure 3-1. *Popfly block building space*

Finding Blocks

The first thing you need to figure out is what blocks you want to use to create a mashup. You may already have an idea but don't know if there is a service that you can use to create what you want. In this chapter, I am going to create a very simple mashup that will demonstrate the skills you can use to create your own.

The mashup I will be making is a news reader that reads the feed from my blog. Like most blogs, mine (http://blogs.msdn.com/eric_griffin/) syndicates my posts in RSS (refer to Chapter 1), so readers can subscribe to my blog to get my latest posts without having to go to my blog's web page to read it. It is published in XML format and available via URL at http://blogs.msdn.com/eric_griffin/rss.xml. Many readers have their own news readers, but I will be creating a customized reader that displays only my posts.

We will start creating the mashup by searching for a block to read the RSS from my site. To the right of the block building space is the Blocks window (see Figure 3-2)

Figure 3-2. *Blocks window*

At the top of the Blocks window is a search field. Typing **RSS** into the field filters the blocks available to allow you to more easily create mashups that are related to the keyword. Also shown in Figure 3-2, divided into categories, are standard blocks that are built into Popfly (e.g., Live News, MSN News Feeds, News Reader, and RSS), blocks created by me (we will get into that in Chapter 6), and blocks that have been shared by other users.

Look at the block called RSS. Clicking the block gives you further information about the block if you are unsure about its functionality (see Figure 3-3). In this example, we want to retrieve posts from a blog, so select the RSS block.

Figure 3-3. *Selecting a block shows more information.*

Setting Block Properties

Drag the RSS block onto the block building space. After a brief animation, the block appears, and you can drag and drop the block anywhere on the visible canvas. To get more space to work, you can minimize the icon in the upper-left corner of the block window. Hover the mouse over the block on the design surface to see the default operation the block can perform and the default parameters of the operation (see Figure 3-4).

Figure 3-4. *The RSS Block: its operation and default properties*

There are two circles on the right and left sides of the block. These are connectors to other blocks (more on how to do that in the next section). Near the upper-right corner of the block, there is a small panel with three icons. The "X" icon will delete the block from the space. Clicking the light bulb icon will filter the block window as if you typed in the name of the block as a keyword in the search field. The wrench icon will allow you to edit the block's properties.

Click the wrench icon of the RSS block. A zoom animation will occur, and the screen will look like Figure 3-5.

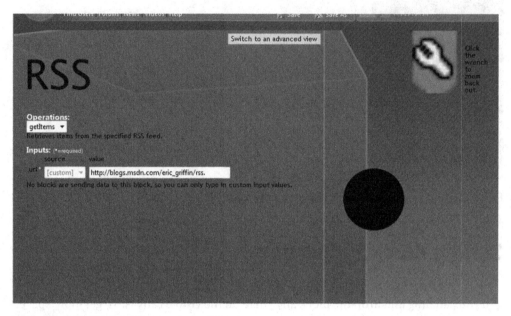

Figure 3-5. *RSS Block getItems properties*

The first thing you will see is the Operations list box in the upper-left corner of the block. There are two operations getItems and getFeed. A short description of the operation is below the list box. Select getItems as the operation that we will execute. The description updates to read, "Retrieves items from the specified RSS feed." The operation getFeed retrieves general information about the feed like the author and URL. This doesn't serve our needs in this example.

Below Operations is the Inputs section; inputs are required for the operation to work. Required fields are indicated with an asterisk and usually have default values. In this case, what is required is the URL of the feed you want to retrieve. The default value for the RSS block is the MSDN blog feed (`http://blogs.msdn.com/MainFeed.aspx`). Type `http://blogs.msdn.com/eric_griffin/rss.xml` into the "value" field.

You will notice that the "source" field is grayed out and disabled. The "source" field is disabled when no block is connecting into the block (i.e., from the left-side connector).

Connecting Blocks

Click the wrench icon to set the operation and the inputs for the RSS block. Return to the block window, and drag and drop a News Reader block onto the design surface to the right of the RSS block (you may have to clear the block search box for News Reader to appear); see Figure 3-6.

Figure 3-6. *The RSS and News Reader blocks*

Each block has an input connector on its left side and an output connector on its right. Connections between blocks are made by joining the output of a block to the input of a second block. Block connectors can receive more than one input. In this case, the "source" list box shown in Figure 3-5 would be enabled, and you would have to choose which incoming block's data to use.

Notice that as soon as you dropped the News Reader block on the design surface, a preview of what the control looks like (with some default data) displays in the background.

Click the right connector of the RSS block. The available block connection points will be highlighted in yellow (see Figure 3-7). A line appears as you move the mouse to a block connector. Click the News Reader block's connector to set the connection.

Click the wrench on the News Reader to set its properties. The News Reader has only one operation, so only addNewsItem is visible, with the description of "Adds a news item." See Figure 3-8.

If you ever need to delete a connection between blocks, just click the connecting line.

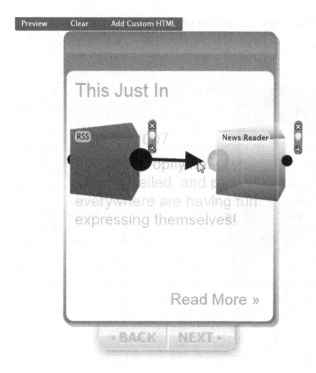

Figure 3-7. *Connecting the RSS and News Reader blocks*

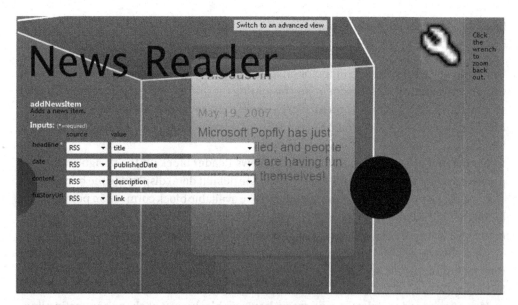

Figure 3-8. *News Reader block properties and operations*

Since there is only one input block, the News Reader selects the RSS block as the default input for all of the source fields for each input. Selecting one of the "value" list boxes reveals many data fields that are passed by the RSS block. The News Reader, however, has fields for the title, publication date, description, and link. The News Reader block recognizes those fields and automatically selects defaults values for them. I will go over more of how blocks define and recognize data in Chapter 5.

Viewing Advanced Properties

Before we test the mashup, let's look at what is happening behind the scenes. While you are viewing the sources and values of the News Reader, click the "Switch to an advanced view" button at the top of the block. If you are familiar with JavaScript, you will recognize the code shown in Figure 3-9. Experienced JavaScript users can add new code or adjust the code generated for the News Reader block. It is important to fully understand block architecture before making changes in the advanced view (more on that in Chapter 7). Editing the code in advanced view turns the color of the block gray. You don't want make changes, so click "Go back to the simple view".

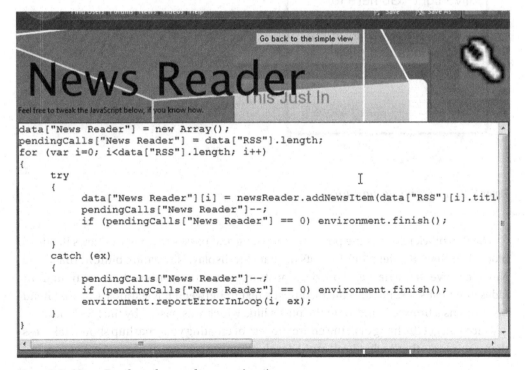

Figure 3-9. *News Reader advanced properties view*

Testing Your Mashup

Now that we've connected the RSS and News Reader blocks and set their operations and inputs, we are ready to test the mashup. Click the wrench icon to go back to the mashup design space, and click the Preview menu item at the top of the design surface. The design surface and Blocks windows slide away. A notice, framed in yellow, may appear stating "Retrieving data from `http://blogs.msdn.com/eric_griffin/rss.xml`..." before the mashup appears (see Figure 3-10).

Figure 3-10. *The running mashup*

The RSS block retrieves the posts from my blog and passes them to the News Reader block. The News Reader block formats the data for display. Navigation buttons (Back and Next) to move to the next and previous posts appear at the bottom. A clever animation fades one post's text out and the next post's text in between navigations. Clicking Read More opens a browser window to the post's link, which was passed by the RSS block.

Once you get the hang of it, the entire process of creating your mashup should take less than a minute—that's what I call rapid development.

Adding HTML to Your Mashup

You've got your mashup up and running, but suppose you want to add a little more to it. If you are comfortable with HTML, you can easily add it to your mashup. Click the Customize menu item at the bottom of the preview to return to the design surface. Click the Add Custom HTML to see a text area for you to type HTML markup; see Figure 3-11.

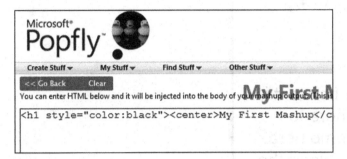

Figure 3-11. *Adding custom HTML*

If you type text into this area without markup, the text will appear in the background of the mashup with no styling. Using HTML tags gives you greater control and flexibility of the content that will appear. Type **<h1 style="color:black"><center>My First Mashup!<center></h1>** into the text area (see Figure 3-11). The h1 tag is an HTML tag that represents the font style Header 1. Using it in this code formats the text to appear larger and bolder than surrounding text. The style attribute sets the color of the font to black (by default, the font color is white). The center tag centers the text on the page. Without enclosing the text in this tag, the text would be aligned at the far right.

Click the Go Back menu item to save the HTML. Click Preview to test the mashup again. As Figure 3-12 shows, the HTML appears centered, like the News Reader, on the page.

My First Mashup

HTML Textblock for Silverlight

Tue, 11 Sep 2007

Need to display rich text in Silverlight? Go here to check out the demo here. click here to download the source code and play around with it yourself!

Read More »

Figure 3-12. *The results of adding Custom HTML*

Saving Your Mashup

Now that you have completed your mashup, you can save it by clicking the Save or Save As button. A dialog box will appear asking you to name the mashup. Type **My First Mashup** in the box (spaces are allowed in your mashup name), and click the Accept and Save button (see Figure 3-13).

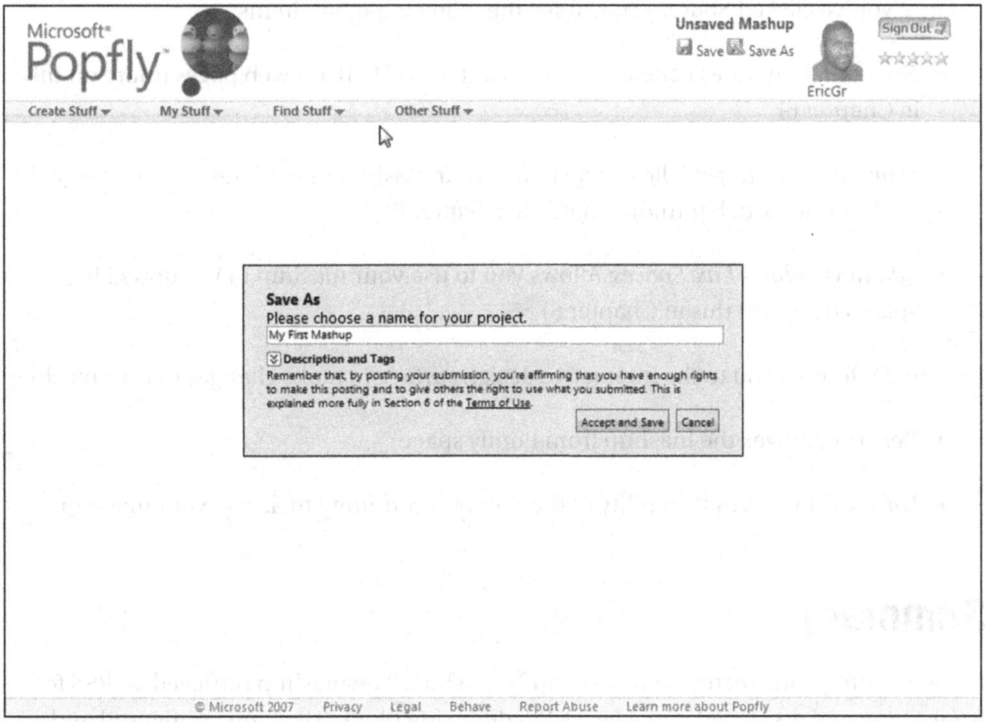

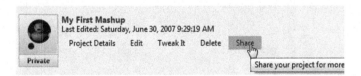

Figure 3-15. *Save dialog box*

Sharing Your Popfly Mashup

You can publish your mashup, so the community can see and rate it.

Select My Stuff ➤ My Projects. Select Share from the My First Mashup project menu (see Figure 3-16).

Figure 3-16. *Sharing a mashup*

Once you've clicked Share, you will see the following menu items:

- *Embed it*: Generates code for you to insert into HTML on web pages (more on this in Chapter 6)

- *Download as Gadget*: Allows you to use your mashup as a Windows Vista gadget in the Windows sidebar (more on this in Chapter 6)

- *Add to Windows Live Spaces*: Allows you to use your mashup in Windows Live Spaces (more on this in Chapter 6)

- *Edit*: Returns you to the interactive design surface to make changes to your mashup

- *Delete*: Removes the mashup from Popfly space

- *Unshare*: Removes the ability of the Popfly community to access your mashup

Summary

In this chapter, you created your first Popfly mashup. The mashup retrieved an RSS feed from a blog and displayed it in a News Reader using blocks that you configured and connected in Popfly's block design surface. You also added HTML to your mashup page. You shared it with the Popfly community so that members can see, rate, and mix your mashup.

■ ■ ■

CHAPTER 4

More Mashup Examples

In Chapter 3, you created your first mashup. The mashup retrieved an RSS feed from a blog and displayed it in a News Reader using blocks that you configured and connected in Popfly's block design surface. You also added HTML to your mashup and shared it with the Popfly community so members can see, rate, and mix your mashup.

In this chapter, you will create three more mashups that will explore other Popfly blocks that use photos and maps.

Creating a Flickr Mashup

Flickr (http://www.flickr.com) is a photo-sharing web site and web services suite and an online community platform, and it's an early example of a Web 2.0 application. In March 2005, Yahoo Inc. acquired Ludicorp, the company that created Flickr.

Flickr enables its users to upload, share, and tag their photos. Tagging is a form of categorizing. For example, a user with uploaded photos about a trip to the beach can tag the photos "Fun at the Beach" or "Beach" or "Family Time." Since everyone's experiences are different, simple phrases or words can describe an interesting variety of pictures.

This mashup will allow users to search the millions of photos within Flickr by tags.

Getting a Flickr Account

To create this mashup, you need a Flickr account. You can get one by going to Flickr's home page (http://www.flickr.com). Click Create an Account, and enter an existing Yahoo ID or create a new one.

After you create your account, you can upload and tag your own photos. For the purposes of creating this mashup, I won't be covering that here. There are already millions of photos we can search.

Setting Up Your Flickr Mashup

Once you have a Flickr account set up, you're ready to start creating your mashup in Popfly. You'll add three blocks: Flickr, User Input, and PhotoSphere.

Adding the Flickr Block

Start by creating a new mashup and adding the Flickr block:

1. Select Create Stuff ➤ Mashup to get a clean mashup design surface to appear.

2. Go to the Block window, and type **Flickr** in the search box. Drag and drop the Flickr block onto the design surface (see Figure 4-1).

Figure 4-1. *The Flickr block with a missing API key*

3. Below the Flickr block, you will see a label saying Missing Key. As I stated in Chapter 1, many providers require the user to have a unique API key to use their services. Flickr requires that you have a key so that the company can track usage and prevent abuse of its service. Popfly blocks that require a key will display this label. Click the label to display a dialog box (see Figure 4-2) with information on how to obtain a key.

4. Once you have an API key, you can use Flickr services under the terms and conditions stipulated by Flickr. Copy the Key information shown in Figure 4-3 into the dialog box in Figure 4-2, and click the Update button.

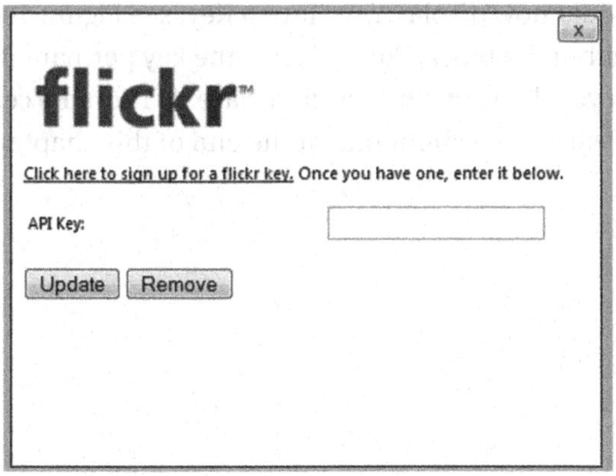

Figure 4-2. *Flickr API key dialog box*

5. Within the dialog box is a link that will send you to the service's web site to obtain the key. Click the "Click here to sign up for a flickr key" link. Your browser should open to Flickr's API application page. Fill out the required information, and your key will be generated. Figure 4-3 shows my API key (I have changed the number, because it is uniquely assigned to me).

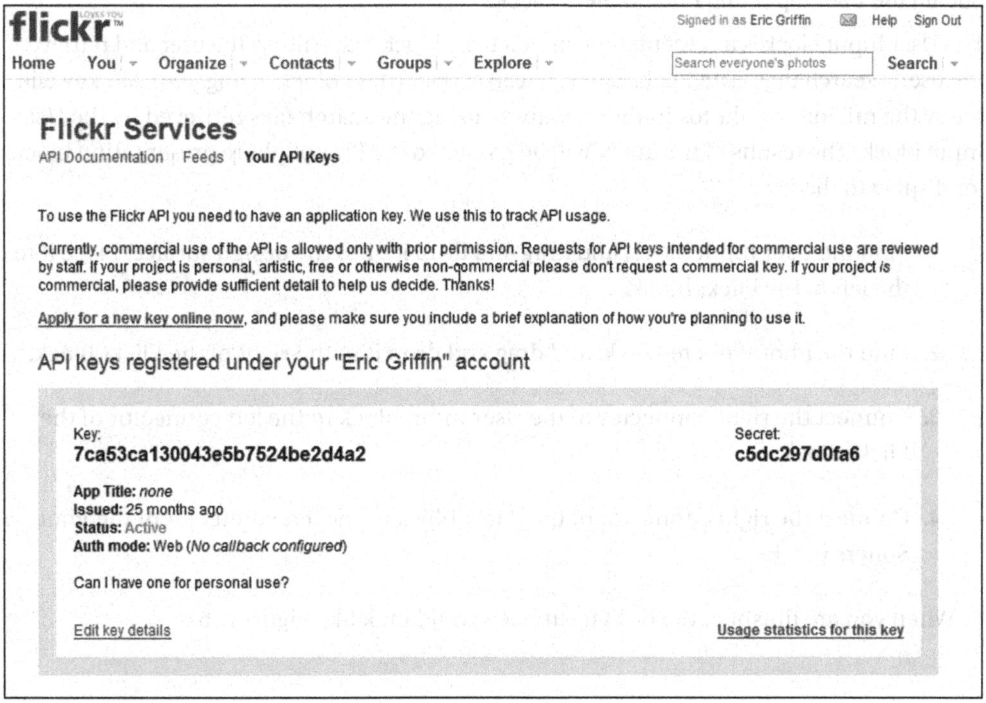

Figure 4-3. *Flickr API key*

6. The label under the block should now display You Have a Key; see Figure 4-4. In addition to storing the key within the block, Popfly stores the key permanently for future use by Flickr blocks that you drag onto the design surface. API keys are centrally managed by Popfly. You can learn more about that at the end of this chapter.

Figure 4-4. *Flickr block with API key*

Now that you have your Flickr API enabled, you can add the other two blocks: User Input and PhotoSphere.

Adding the User Input and PhotoSphere Blocks

The User Input block is a presentation/interactivity block that will ask the user and retrieve the user's search tags. The Flickr block, a web service/data block, using your API key will query the millions of photos in their database using the search tags retrieved by the User Input block. The results of the query will be passed to the PhotoSphere presentation block for display to the user.

1. Find the User Input block, and drag and drop it onto the design surface. Place it to the left of the Flickr block.

2. Find the PhotoSphere block, and drag and drop it to the right of the Flickr block.

3. Connect the right connector of the User Input block to the left connector of the Flickr block.

4. Connect the right connector of the Flickr block to the left connector of the Photo-Sphere block.

When you are finished, the design surface should look like Figure 4-5.

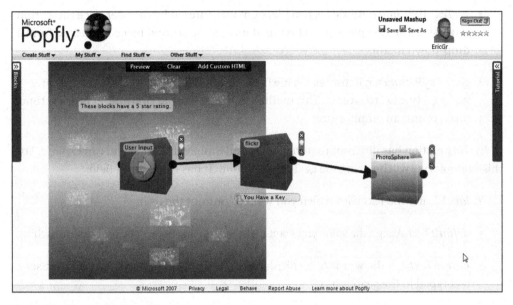

Figure 4-5. *Photo mashup blocks*

Setting the User Input Block Properties

The User Input block has several operations:

- *getText*: Retrieves text typed in by the user once the button created with the User Input block is clicked.

- *getTwoTextValues*: Retrieves two pieces of text typed in by the user once the button is clicked.

- *getThreeTextValues*: Retrieves three pieces of text typed in by the user once the button is clicked.

- *getChoiceFromDropDown*: Retrieves text selected from a drop-down menu by the user. Once the button is clicked, the selection is retrieved.

- *getTwoChoicesFromDropDown*: Retrieves two pieces of text selected by the user once the button is clicked.

- *getThreeChoicesFromDropDown*: Retrieves three pieces of text selected by the user once the button is clicked.

- *getTextAndChoice*: Retrieves two pieces of text entered by the user once the button is clicked. The first piece of text is typed in, and the second piece is selected from a drop-down menu.

- *getQueryParameter*: Retrieves a value from the query string in the URL (e.g., `http://www.popfly.ms/?foo=test`). This method will only work at runtime; at preview time, it will return an empty string.

Each operation has different required fields and input values that you can explore. For this example, we will be using the getText operation. It has three input fields:

- *label*: Enter the text with which you want to prompt the user.

- *defaultText*: Assign the value you want in the search box before the user types anything.

- *buttonText*: Set the words to be displayed on the button that will retrieve the user's text typed in the search box.

Set the User Input block properties as follows:

1. Type **Enter Tags** in the value field for label.

2. Leave the defaultText field blank.

3. Type **Search Flickr** in the buttonText value field.

Figure 4-6 shows the User Input block properties set for this example.

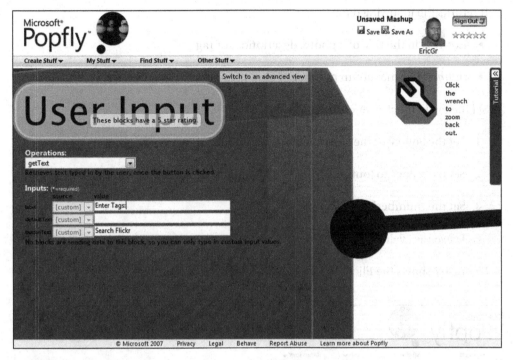

Figure 4-6. *Setting User Input properties*

Setting the Flickr Block Properties

The Flickr block has five operations:

- *getGeoTaggedPhotos*: Get photos that have been labeled with a latitude and longitude location on the earth.

- *getPhotos*: Retrieve photos by their tags.

- *getTags*: Retrieve the tags for a specified photo.

- *getUserPhotos*: Get the photos for a specified Flickr user.

- *getPhotoSet*: Get a Flickr photo set.

For this example, we will be using getPhotos. It has two fields:

- *text*: Text in the title of a photo, description, or tag

- *number*: The maximum number of photos to return

It returns the following data:

- *text*: Text in the title of a photo, description, or tag

- *number*: The maximum number of photos to return

Set the Flickr block properties as follows:

1. Set the Source of the "text" field to User Input.

2. Set its "value" to [output string], which should be done by default.

3. Set the "number" field's Source to [custom].

4. Leave the "value" field blank.

Figure 4-7 shows the Flickr block properties set for this example.

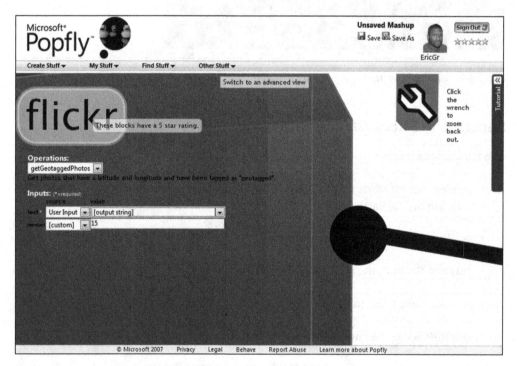

Figure 4-7. *Setting Flickr block properties*

Setting the PhotoSphere Block Properties

The PhotoSphere block has only the addImage operation, which can receive one or more images from the Flickr block. It has two fields:

- *url*: The URL pointing to an image

- *title*: A caption for the image

Set the PhotoSphere block properties as follows:

1. Set the "url source" to "flickr" and the "value" to "url".

2. Set the "title source" to "flickr" and the "value" to "title".

Figure 4-8 shows the PhotoSphere block properties set for this example.

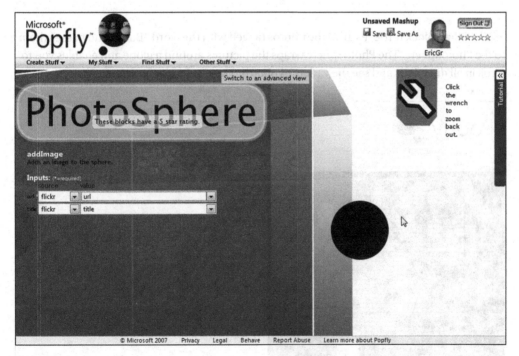

Figure 4-8. *PhotsoSphere block properties*

Previewing the Flickr Mashup

Now, take a look at the Flickr completed mashup:

1. Click the Preview menu on the design surface.

2. Once the mashup displays, type **Baby** into the search box after the Enter Tags label, as shown in Figure 4-9.

3. Click the Search Flickr button.

Figure 4-9. *Entering tags*

The Flickr block retrieves all of the photos tagged with the word "Baby" and passes them to the PhotoSphere. The PhotoSphere wraps the pictures around a globe and enables you to scroll in all directions and see the variety of photos. The results can be seen in Figure 4-10.

Figure 4-10. *The Flickr mashup*

Saving Your Mashup

Finish up by saving your mashup.

1. Click Save.

2. Name the mashup "My Photo Mashup".

You can decide if you want to share your mashup with the Popfly community.

Creating a Virtual Earth Mashup

Mapping mashups are the most common type. Mapping applications display a specific location on a map based on longitude and latitude. Most people don't know the longitude and latitude of cities, towns, and countries, so services exist to embed the mapping applications with that data. The embedding process is called geotagging, or sometimes geoencoding, and it allows you to add geographical identification metadata to various media such as web sites, RSS feeds, or images. In addition to latitude and longitude coordinates, this data can also include altitudes and place names.

In this example, we will be using Virtual Earth and information from Yahoo's Upcoming.com (a service that tracks events throughout the United States with geoencoding).

Getting an Upcoming Account

As with the Flickr mashup, Yahoo's Upcoming.com service requires that you have an API key to use its web services. You can sign up for the Upcoming service at `http://upcoming.yahoo.com/`; see Figure 4-11.

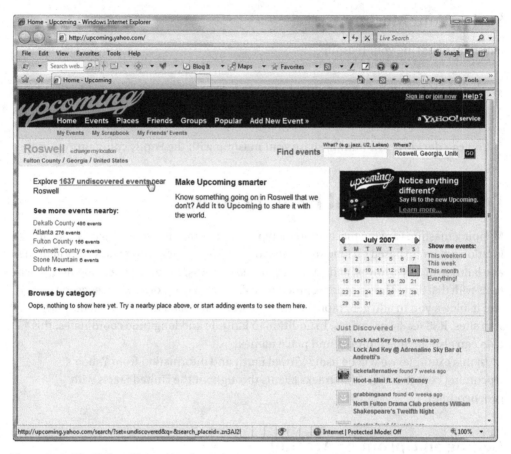

Figure 4-11. *The Yahoo Upcoming home page*

After you have your account, you can generate an API key for use in the Popfly block. You can read more about the API at http://upcoming.yahoo.com/services/api/. Click Get/Check Your API Key to generate an API key at http://upcoming.yahoo.com/services/api/keygen.php. Figure 4-12 shows the generated API page.

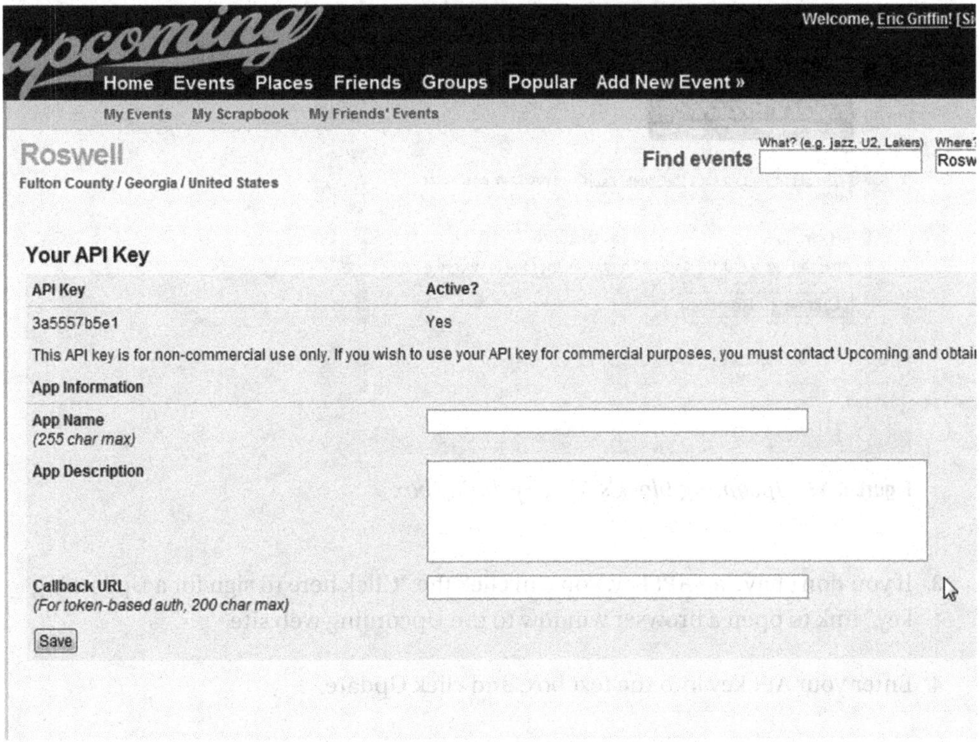

Figure 4-12. *API key page at Upcoming.com*

Getting Started on Your Upcoming Virtual Earth Mashup

Once you have your API key, you're ready to start. Return to Popfly and log in.

1. Start a new mashup by selecting My Stuff ➤ My Projects. Select Build Stuff ➤ Create a Mashup to get a new clean mashup design surface to appear.

2. Go to the Block List, and type **Upcoming** in the search box. Drag and drop the Upcoming block onto the design surface (see Figure 4-13). The Upcoming block requires an API key, so you will see a label below the block stating Missing Key. Click the label to open the block's key dialog box (see Figure 4-13).

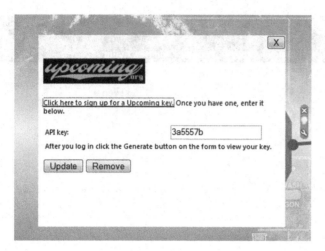

Figure 4-13. *Upcoming block's API Key dialog box*

3. If you don't have an API key, you can click the "Click here to sign for a Upcoming key" link to open a browser window to the Upcoming web site.

4. Enter your API key into the text box, and click Update.

Setting the Upcoming Block Properties

After you have entered the API key, you are ready to set the Upcoming block properties. It has one operation:

- *findEvents*: Used to find events from the Upcoming service

It has one field:

- *searchText*: Enter the text for the search as if you were on the Upcoming web site.

In this example, we want to find all of the events in Upcoming that are related to music. Type **music** into the "value" field of the Upcoming block, as shown in Figure 4-14.

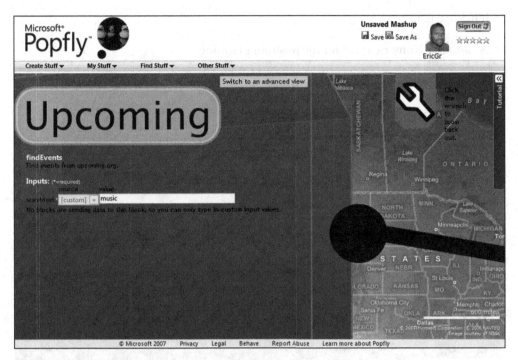

Figure 4-14. *Upcoming block properties and operation*

Setting the Virtual Earth Block Properties

Now that you've got your Upcoming block, complete with API key, added to the design surface, it's time to configure the Virtual Earth block's properties. This block (see Figure 4-15) has four operations:

- *addPushpin*: Adds a pushpin to the map at a specific location

- *setMapView*: Sets the viewable area of the map

- *drawLine*: Draws a line from point to point on the map

- *deleteAllPushpins*: Removes all pushpins from the map

It has five fields:

- *latitude*: Numeric value for the pushpin's latitude

- *longitude*: Numeric value for the pushpin's longitude

- *url*: The web location for the pushpin's image

- *title*: The pushpin's title

- *description*: The pushpin's description representing the location

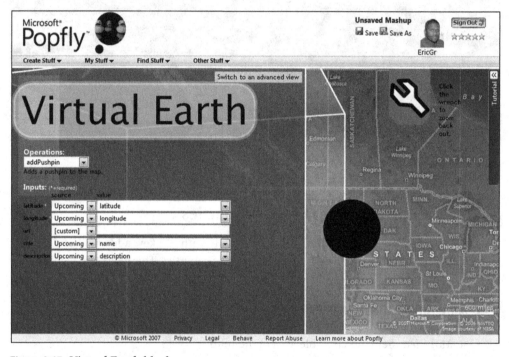

Figure 4-15. *Virtual Earth block*

Follow these steps to configure the properties:

1. Drag and drop the Virtual Earth block from the block window to the right of the Upcoming block. You will see a map of the United States appear in the background of the design surface.

Note The Virtual Earth block is a presentation block. You can't have more than one presentation block on the design surface. If you try to drag another Virtual Earth block onto the design surface, Popfly will display an error.

---

2. Connect the two blocks by clicking the right connector on the Upcoming block and dragging the line over to the left connector on the Virtual Earth

3. Select addPushpin from the Operations drop-down menu.

4. Because you've only connected the Upcoming block, the Source drop-down menus are set to it by default. You should also see the two values automatically selected by looking at the properties passed by Upcoming: "latitude" is selected for the "latitude" field and "longitude" is selected for the "longitude" field. In the "title" field, select "Upcoming" as the "source" and "name" as the "value". In the "description" field, select "Upcoming" as the source and "description" as the value.

5. Return to the design surface, and click Preview. The music events in Upcoming are retrieved, and a pushpin is added for each event's location (see Figure 4-16). If you hover over the pushpin, the title and description are displayed.

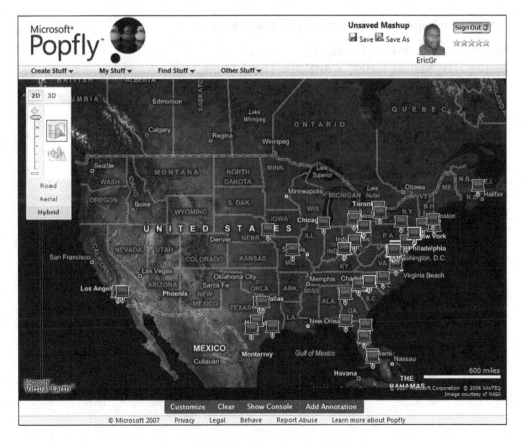

Figure 4-16. *The Upcoming Virtual Earth mashup in the default view*

Customizing the Virtual Earth Block

The Virtual Earth block focuses on the United States by default, so it's great if you want to see all of the events in the United States, but you're probably interested in events only in your local area. We are going to use some of the advanced capabilities of blocks to set the map to a particular location.

Setting the Location of the Virtual Earth Block

We will set the location to the San Francisco area:

1. Click Customize to return to the design surface.

2. Open the properties of the Virtual Earth block by clicking the wrench.

3. Click the Advanced View label to display the code in Listing 4-1.

Listing 4-1. *Default Code in the Virtual Earth Block Advanced View*

```
data["Virtual Earth"] = new Array();
pendingCalls["Virtual Earth"] = data["Upcoming"].length;
for (var i=0; i<data["Upcoming"].length; i++)
{
    try
    {

        data["Virtual Earth"][i] = virtualEarth.addPushpin(~CCC
data["Upcoming"][i].latitude,
data["Upcoming"][i].longitude, "", data["Upcoming"][i].name, ~CCC
data["Upcoming"][i].description);
        pendingCalls["Virtual Earth"]--;
        if (pendingCalls["Virtual Earth"] == 0) environment.finish();

    }
    catch (ex)
    {
        pendingCalls["Virtual Earth"]--;
        if (pendingCalls["Virtual Earth"] == 0) environment.finish();
        environment.reportErrorInLoop(i, ex);
    }
}
```

The code is generated automatically when the Upcoming block is connected to the Virtual Earth block. We don't want to change any of pregenerated JavaScript code, but we will add to it. The most important block of code is the JavaScript within the try block. The try block is a way to trap errors. The code after the word "try," and enclosed in between the curly braces ({}) is the heart of the block execution and where we want to add our code. The catch block will be executed if an error occurs.

Configuring the Parameters of the Virtual Earth Block

We will be using the setMapView function. Though it has seven parameters, we will be using only two: latitude and longitude. In order to set the map to the correct location, we need the longitude and latitude of San Francisco. You can find the location on the Internet in various locations; see the "Geoencoding Resources" sidebar for more information.

GEOENCODING RESOURCES

Many web sites allow you to search for longitude and latitude of locations around the world. Here is a list of resources on the Web:

- *Latitude and Longitude of World Cities* provides a list of world locations' coordinates at `http://www.infoplease.com/ipa/A0001769.html`.

- *Look-up Latitude and Longitude—USA* provides a list of United States city geoencoding information by state at `http://www.bcca.org/misc/qiblih/latlong_us.html`.

- *Latitude and Longitude* allows you to find coordinates of cities/towns, landmarks, and more at `http://www.factmonster.com/atlas/latitude-longitude.html`.

Configuring setMapView

After finding that the location of San Francisco is 33 degrees latitude by –84 degrees longitude, we now have the information we need to call the function.

1. setMapView takes five fields in the following order; enter the data as shown:

   - *latitude*: The latitude of the center of the map. Set it to **33**.

   - *longitude*: The longitude of the center of the map. Set it to **–84**.

   - *zoom*: The zoom level of the map. Leave it blank for the default height.

   - *altitude*: The altitude, in meters, above the ground. Leave it blank for the default altitude.

- *pitch*: The angle of the view for 3-D settings. Set it to –90.

- *heading*: Used if you are using Virtual Earth's 3-D settings. Leave blank for the default heading.

2. Type the code in Listing 4-2 below try and {.

Listing 4-2. *Code to Add to the Virtual Earth Block Advanced View*

```
virtualEarth.setMapView(33,-84, "","","", -90,"");
```

Figure 4-17 shows the final code.

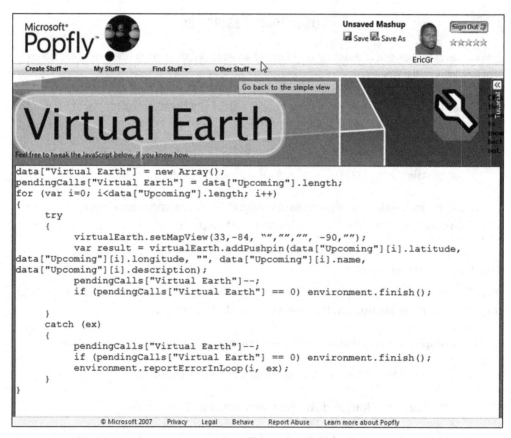

Figure 4-17. *Editing the Virtual Earth code in the Advanced view*

Displaying San Francisco in the Virtual Earth Block

Now that you've got the setMapView parameters set, follow these steps to complete your mashup:

1. Click the wrench icon to return to the design surface. The Virtual Earth block is colored gray, indicating that it has been modified with custom code.

2. Click Preview to see the mashup (see Figure 4-18). Virtual Earth is focused on northern California. Hover the mouse over the pushpins to see the events in that location.

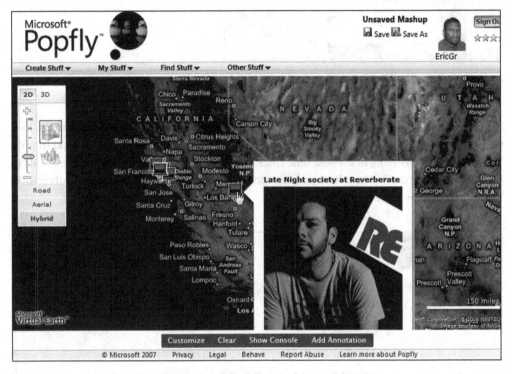

Figure 4-18. *Upcoming Virtual Earth mashup focused on California*

You can further customize this mashup by adding the User Input block and connecting it to the Upcoming block to allow the user to search for events.

Managing Your API Keys

In the examples in this chapter, you were shown how to use an API key with Flickr and Upcoming blocks. The API keys were also stored by Popfly. You can access all of your API keys from different vendors by selecting Main Menu ➤ My Projects ➤ My Stuff ➤ Developer Keys; see Figure 4-19.

Figure 4-19. *Selecting Developer Keys*

A page containing a list of your API keys will be displayed. Select an API key from the list on the right; for example, Figure 4-20 shows the Flickr key you entered in the Flickr block. You can edit the API Key in the text box. Click Update to store the text box contents. Click Remove to delete the API key. Remember, updating or removing the API key will affect any block with the key stored in it.

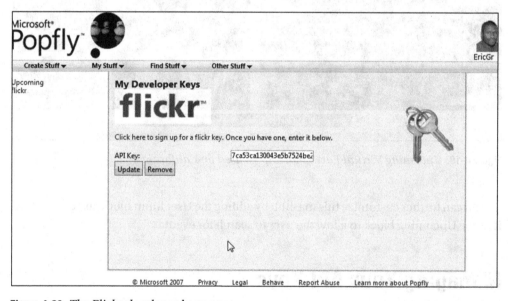

Figure 4-20. *The Flickr developer key page*

You can update or remove the Flickr API key by selecting My Stuff ➤ Developer Keys.

Summary

In this chapter, you've created two more mashups: one using Flickr's photo service block and the PhotoSphere block. You've also created one using the Upcoming service with Virtual Earth. You've learned how to generate and manage API keys and how to add custom code to modify a block. You've also learned how to use the User Input block to retrieve information from the user and pass it on to blocks.

In the next chapter, we will explore web page creation using the Popfly Web Page Creator.

CHAPTER 5

■■■

Creating Web Pages

In Chapter 4, you further explored creating Popfly mashups by creating a photo mashup using Flickr and a map mashup using Yahoo's Upcoming Event service with Microsoft's Virtual Earth.

In this chapter, we are going to switch gears and look at the web page creation features in Popfly. The Web Page Creator provides everything you would expect from an HTML editor, including the ability to create hyperlinks, embed images, and change page styles. It also has the added functionality of enabling you to embed your Popfly mashups. After you have finished with your page, you can share it, so the rest of the community or external users can see and experience it.

You've created several mashups in the previous chapters, and each mashup could be individually published on a separate page. In this chapter, we are going to create a page that has all three mashups and share it with the Popfly community and the Internet at large.

Creating Your First Page

The Popfly Web Page Creator can be accessed by selecting Main Menu ➤ Create Stuff ➤ Web Page. The new unsaved page is created and displayed in the Web Page Creator (see Figure 5-1). Hidden, to the right, is the Web Page Creator Tutorial window. You can expand it by clicking the "<<" icon or Show Tutorial link.

The page is titled Unsaved Web Page. To the upper right, you'll find three buttons with options for the current page: Preview, Save, and Save As (see Figure 5-2).

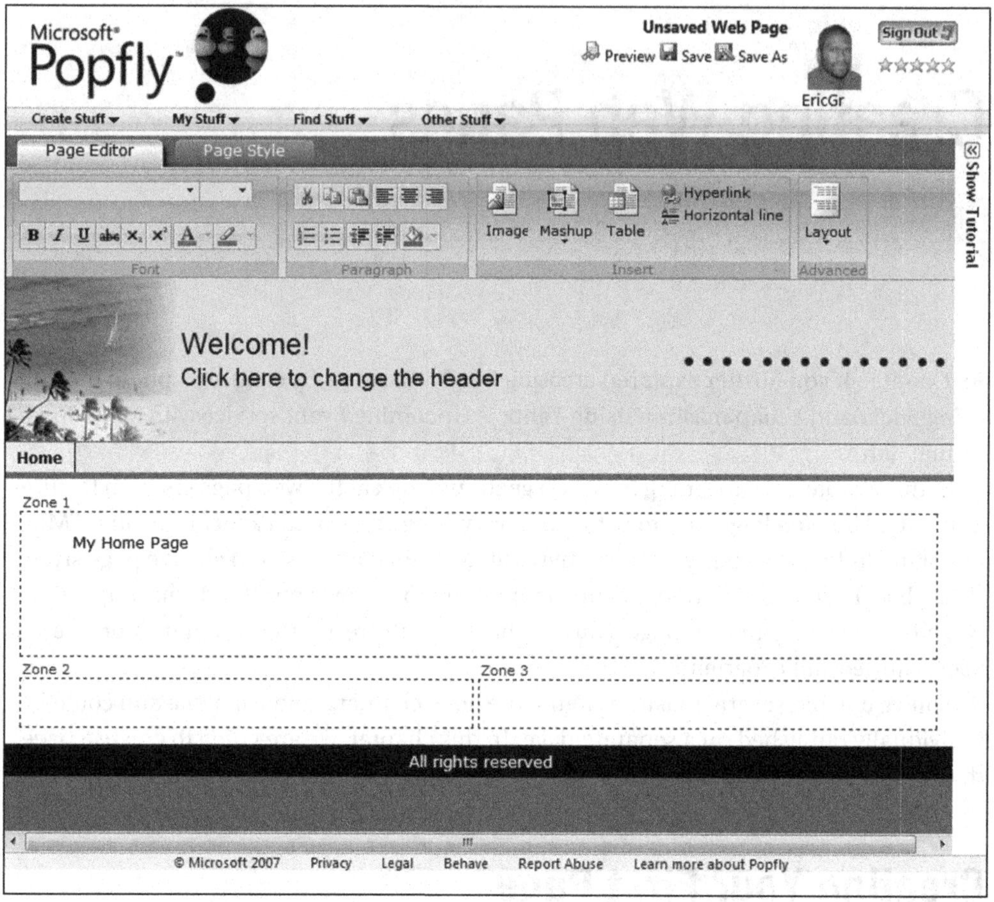

Figure 5-1. *The Web Page Creator*

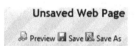

Figure 5-2. *The Preview, Save, and Save As buttons*

The Save and Save As buttons function in the way you'd expect them to: the Save As button allows you to save the page and change its name, and the Save button saves the page with its current name. Click the Save As button, and the Save As dialog box appears (see Figure 5-3).

Type **My Mashup Page** in the text box, and click the Accept and Save button. Remember to click the Terms of Use link to look at the terms. After a few moments, the page is saved, and you are returned to the Page Editor.

Save As

Please choose a name for your project.

My Mashup Page

⊻ Description and Tags

Remember that, by posting your submission, you're affirming that you have
enough rights to make this posting and to give others the right to use what
you submitted. This is explained more fully in Section 6 of the <u>Terms of Use</u>.

Accept and Save   Cancel

Figure 5-3. *The Save As dialog box*

Changing Headers and Footers

The first thing we are going to do is set up the headers and footers for the page. Click the
Preview button to see the page shown in Figure 5-4. The new page opens and displays the
default content.

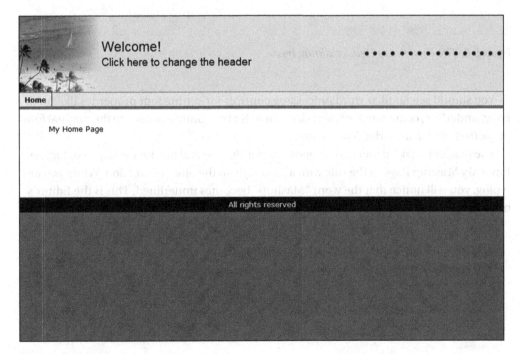

Welcome!
Click here to change the header

Home

My Home Page

Figure 5-4. *A preview of the default page*

We'll get started customizing the page by changing the header. Return to the Page
Editor by closing the preview window. Looking at the header at the top of the page

(see Figure 5-1), you will see the words "Welcome!" and "Click here to change the header." Click the words to open the Customize Header dialog box shown in Figure 5-5.

Figure 5-5. *The Customize Header dialog box*

You should see familiar word processing controls for setting font properties like bold, italic, underline, color, typeface, and size. There is also a button to restore the original font properties, which are Arial, 5 point size.

The header is divided into two sections: one for the title and one for the slogan or tagline. Enter **My Mashup Page** in the title with a bold style in the Site Title section. While you are typing, you will notice that the word "Mashup" becomes underlined. This is the Editor's built-in spell checker at work (see Figure 5-6).

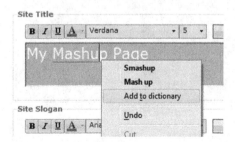

Figure 5-6. *Spellchecking in the editor*

Right-click the word "Mashup," and select "Add to dictionary" to prevent it from being highlighted as a misspelling later. Don't forget to bold the text by selecting the words and clicking the bold button at the top of the section.

You can also change the site slogan. Click in the lower pane of the Customize Header window, and type a site slogan in the bottom editor like "Check out the kools mashups I have created". You shouldn't see the word "Mashups" highlighted, because it's been added to the dictionary (although the word "kools" will be highlighted as a misspelling if you type it). Click OK to save the changes to the page.

It's also possible to change the page footer in the same way. Click the "All rights reserved" text at the bottom of the page. The Customize Footer dialog box appears, as shown in Figure 5-7.

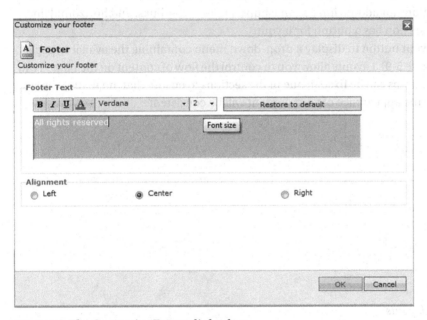

Figure 5-7. *The Customize Footer dialog box*

In this dialog box, you have the same word processing controls and the ability to set the alignment of the content to the left, center (the default), or right. Change the text to whatever you like, and click the OK button to save the changes.

Creating and Adding Content

So far, we have done some basic changes. The editor has a rich set of options available to customize the look and feel of your page. Before we move on with further customizations, let's examine the options that are available to you in the Page Editor and Page Styles tabs.

Let's look at the Page Editor tab, shown in Figure 5-8.

Figure 5-8. *The Page Editor tab*

In the Font section of the tab, you have familiar word processing controls. The controls apply to the text that is contained in the page and the current selection. The Paragraph section contains more word processing controls: cut, copy, paste, left align, center align, right align, bullets, decrease and increase indenting, and background color. The Insert section has buttons for adding images, mashups, tables, hyperlinks, and horizontal lines. The Advanced section has a button for layout.

Click the Layout button to display a drop-down menu containing the available page layouts (see Figure 5-9). Layouts allow you to control the flow of content on the page. Text, images, and mashups can be fixed in one of the sections to ensure that, no matter the size of the browser, the appearance of your content will be consistent.

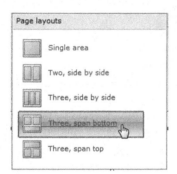

Figure 5-9. *Page layouts*

Select "Three, span bottom" to set the layout to three zones named Zone 1, Zone 2, and Zone 3 corresponding to the sections in the layout.

Click the mouse in Zone 1 to set it as the focus. We are going to add an image to the page by clicking the Image button in the Insert section of the Page Editor tab.

The "Pick an image" dialog box appears. There should be no pictures displayed. You can add them by clicking the Upload Pictures button, which opens the Image Uploader dialog box shown in Figure 5-10.

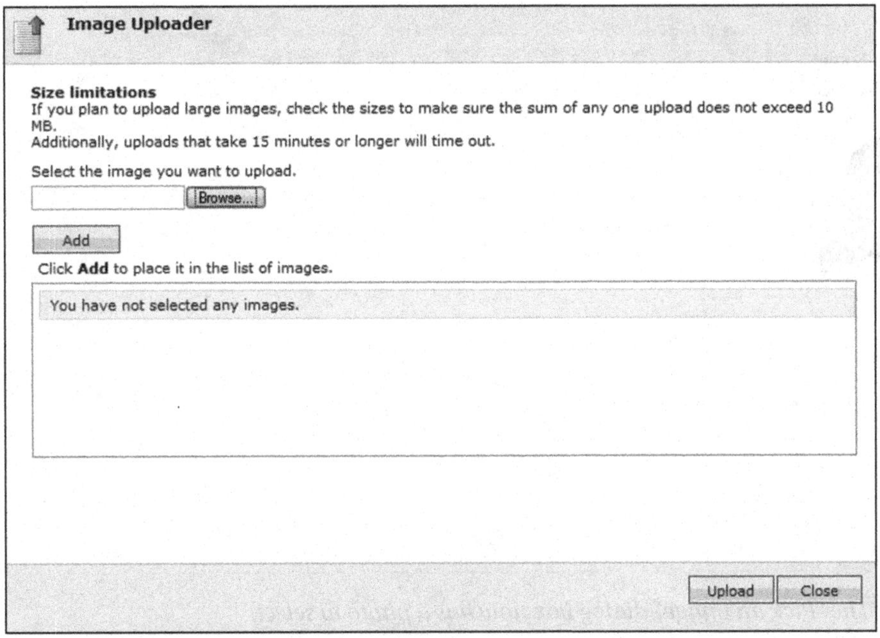

Image Uploader

Size limitations
If you plan to upload large images, check the sizes to make sure the sum of any one upload does not exceed 10 MB.
Additionally, uploads that take 15 minutes or longer will time out.

Select the image you want to upload.

[   ] [Browse...]

[Add]
Click **Add** to place it in the list of images.

You have not selected any images.

[Upload] [Close]

Figure 5-10. *The Image Uploader dialog box*

Click the Browse button to open a Windows Open dialog box to select a picture to add. You can upload image types that browsers can display like GIF, TIF, and JPEG. I found a picture of myself. Click the Open button to return to the Image Uploader dialog box. The text box next to the Browse button should contain the file location of the picture. Click the Add button to place it in the list of images below the button. Next, click Upload to process the images, and click Close to return to the Pick an Image dialog box.

Figure 5-11 shows the image of myself that I uploaded into the Popfly editor.

Select the image you want to add to Zone 1, and click OK to add it. Figure 5-12 shows the image of me in Zone 1 with some text I have added. Note that the image is centered to fit to the square in the preview window, so your images may look distorted.

You can type text into each zone and style it using the controls in the Font and Paragraph sections of the Page Editor tab (refer to Figure 5-8). You can also easily add hyperlinks (as I have done for my blog) by selecting the text the link is attached to and clicking the Hyperlink button in the Insert section of the Page Editor tab. Figure 5-13 shows the Insert Link dialog box that opens.

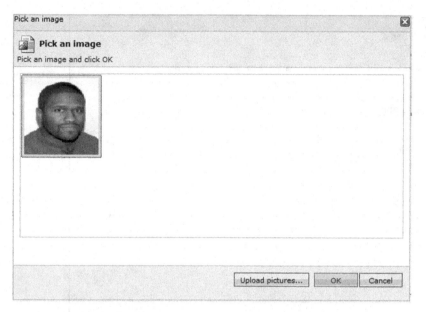

Figure 5-11. *The "Pick an image" dialog box now has a photo to select.*

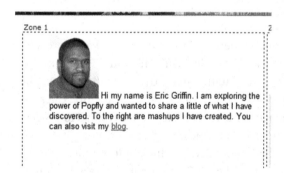

Figure 5-12. *Zone 1 content*

Type the URL you want to attach to the text (in this case, I selected the word "blog" and typed the URL of my blog `http://blogs.msdn.com/eric_griffiin`). Click the OK button to save the link. The selected text will be underlined, and you can navigate to the link in the Page Editor by clicking the link while holding down the Ctrl key.

To edit the link, select the text again, or place the cursor inside the letters of the word and select the Hyperlink button. It will open the Insert Link dialog box shown in Figure 5-13. Change the link, and click OK to save the changes.

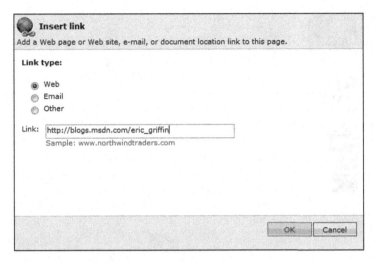

Figure 5-13. *The Insert Link dialog box*

Changing Page Styles

The Page Style tab (see Figure 5-14) gives you many options to customize the look of your page. In the Personalize section, you have buttons to open the Header and Footer customization dialog boxes that we looked at earlier. The Design Options section has buttons for Theme, Style, Navigation, Color, Font, and other general page settings.

Figure 5-14. *The Page Style tab*

We have previously edited the header and footer of the page, so we will move on to the Design Options. Click the Theme button to show a list of available themes. There are dozens to choose from. For this example, select the Computers & Electronics theme category. Select the computer chip image representing a particular theme (see Figure 5-15).

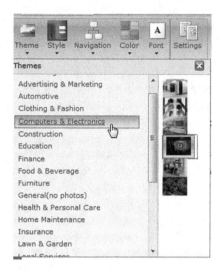

Figure 5-15. *Available themes by category*

Click the Style button to show a menu of available layouts for the site header (see Figure 5-16). Select the one you want to see by clicking it, and the style is applied to the page. I have selected the site header shown in Figure 5-16.

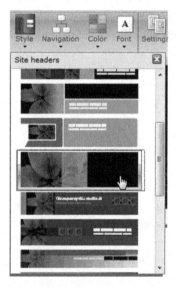

Figure 5-16. *Selecting a site header*

The Navigation button allows you to select where menu links in your page will appear. The options are Left, Top & Left, and Top. Try the various options by selecting each one in turn until you find the one you like. I left the default Top navigation layout.

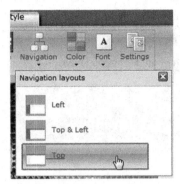

Figure 5-17. *Selecting the Navigation layout*

There are dozens of color-coordinated site color themes available. You can see the entire list by clicking the Color button. I like the Urban colors, so I selected that theme, as shown in Figure 5-18.

Figure 5-18. *Selecting a site color theme*

Now that all of the selections have been made, you can click the Preview button to see the final look and feel of your page. You can see the differences in style from the default page by comparing Figures 5-4 and 5-19.

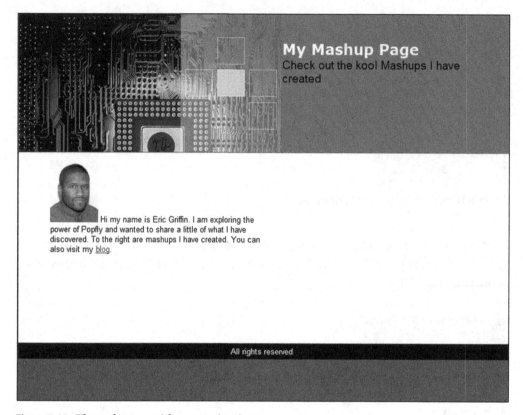

Figure 5-19. *The web page with customizations*

Adding Mashups to Web Pages

The purpose of the page was to show the world our mashups, so we'll explore how to do that now. We will be placing the two mashups that we created earlier in the book in Zone 2 of the page layout, but to have a little more control inside of the zone, we will create a table to contain our mashups. Tables are not only used to contain tabular data but to control positioning of content similar to the zones used in the Popfly editor. This will ensure that the mashups are exactly where we want them.

Close the preview window if it is still open; then, click Zone 2 to make it active. Click the Page Editor tab, and click the Table button. The Create Table dialog box appears, as shown in Figure 5-20.

The dialog box lets you set many options for the table you will be inserting including Color, Color Scheme, Columns, and Rows. A preview area to the right lets you see what your selections will look like before you click OK. The preview is only for the color selection; it does not preview the layout for the number of columns and rows selected.

Create Table   ⊠

🗎 **Create table**
Choose a template and create a table

Select a table type: Parameters: Preview:

Color	Color scheme:	Green ▼
Title and color	Columns:	4
No column titles	Rows:	4
Basic		

Description:
Like the basic table, but
with color.

Note: You **cannot** add more rows
and columns to your table once it is
created.

Preview:

	Column 1	Column 2	Column 3
Row 1			
Row 2			
Row 3			

[OK] [Cancel]

Figure 5-20. *The "Create table" dialog box*

There are four table types to choose from: Color, Title and color, No column titles, and Basic. Click each table type to see what it looks like in the preview area.

I want to display two mashups, one on top of the other. So I'll set the number of columns to 1 and the number of rows to 2. Click OK to show the new table in Zone 2; see Figure 5-21. Insert the cursor above the table, and type **My Mashups**. Increase the font size, and bold the text.

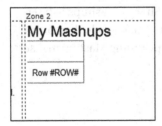

Zone 2

My Mashups

Row #ROW#

Figure 5-21. *The new table in Zone 2*

To resize the table and its rows and columns, double-click one of the cells. Figure 5-22 shows the table after the top row has been double-clicked. You can resize the table by clicking and dragging one of the editing squares on the table. Clicking the circle with the "x" will delete the entire table, if the circle appears on the top of the table. Otherwise, clicking it will delete the cell it is above. Clicking the arrow to the left or right of the circle will add a column to the table. If the arrows are pointing up and down, they will add a row above or below the current cell.

Double-click the cell to activate the editing icons.

Figure 5-22. *Editing a table*

Figure 5-23 shows resizing the table.

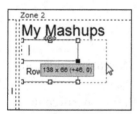

Figure 5-23. *Resizing a table*

Click inside the top part of the table to select that area. Click the Mashup button to show the available mashups. Select My Photo Mashup from the My Shared Mashups list; see Figure 5-24 (note that mashups on a web page must be shared). Click inside the bottom part of the table. If text is there, select and delete it. Select My UpComing Mashup to insert it. Both mashups will be displayed.

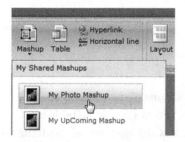

Figure 5-24. *Inserting Mashups*

Click the Preview button to see the final page; see Figure 5-25. Don't forget to save the changes you have made to the page by clicking the Save button at the top of the Page Editor.

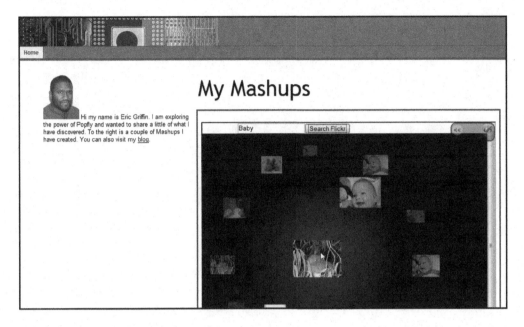

Figure 5-25. *The final My Mashups page*

Summary

In this chapter, you've created your own web page using Popfly's Page Editor. You've learned how to customize pages with styles and layouts and learned how to insert shared mashups for the world to see. In the next chapter, we are going to explore four more ways you can share your mashups with users who are outside of the Popfly community.

CHAPTER 6

■■■

Sharing Your Popfly Mashup

In Chapter 5, you learned how to create pages with the Popfly Page Creator and how to embed your mashup creations in them to share your mashups with the Popfly community. In this chapter, we are going to explore four more ways you can share your mashups—outside of the Popfly community.

Tweaking Your Mashup

Before you show your mashup to the world, you may want to make some minor quick changes. First, you need to choose the mashup to share from among your mashup creations shown by selecting Main Menu ➤ My Stuff ➤ Projects from the main screen. I've chosen to work with the photo mashup we created earlier.

Figure 6-1 shows all of the options available to you once you've selected the mashup: Project Details, Edit, Tweak It, Delete, Share.

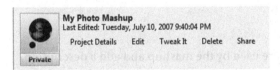

Figure 6-1. *My photo mashup menu options*

The Project Details menu opens the page shown in Figure 6-2.

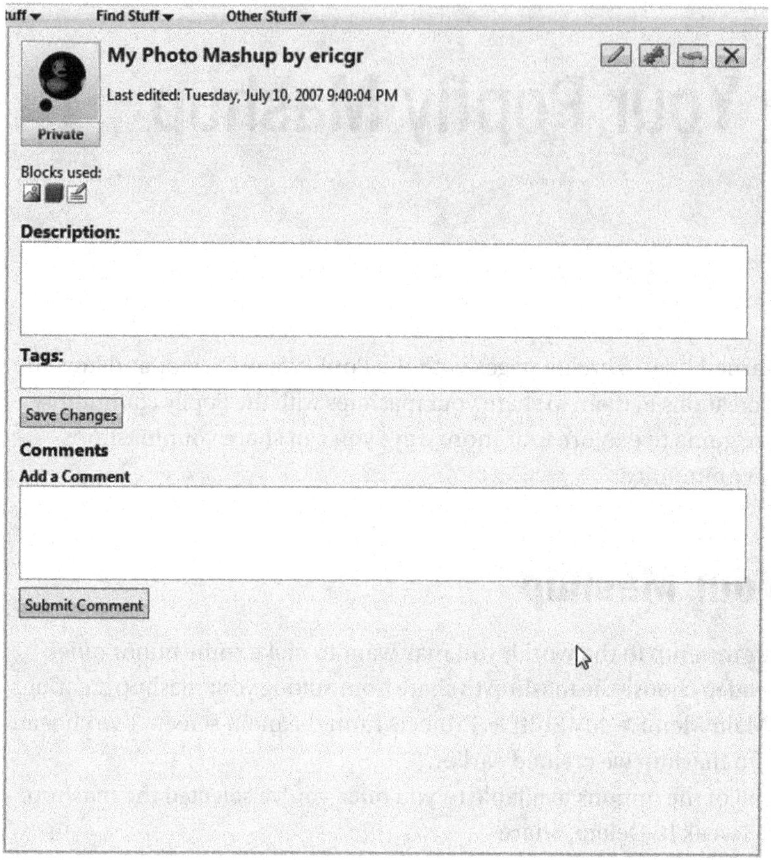

Figure 6-2. *My Photo Mashup Project Details*

On this page, you can see what blocks are used by the mashup and add a description, tags, and comments. In the upper right corner of the page, there are buttons for editing the mashup in the mashup creator, tweaking it, sharing it, and deleting it, respectively. To navigate back to your list of project, click Main Menu ➤ My Stuff ➤ Projects.

Referring to Figure 6-1, click the Tweak It option to open the Tweak It editor shown in Figure 6-3. The Edit option opens the mashup creator, as explained in Chapter 3.

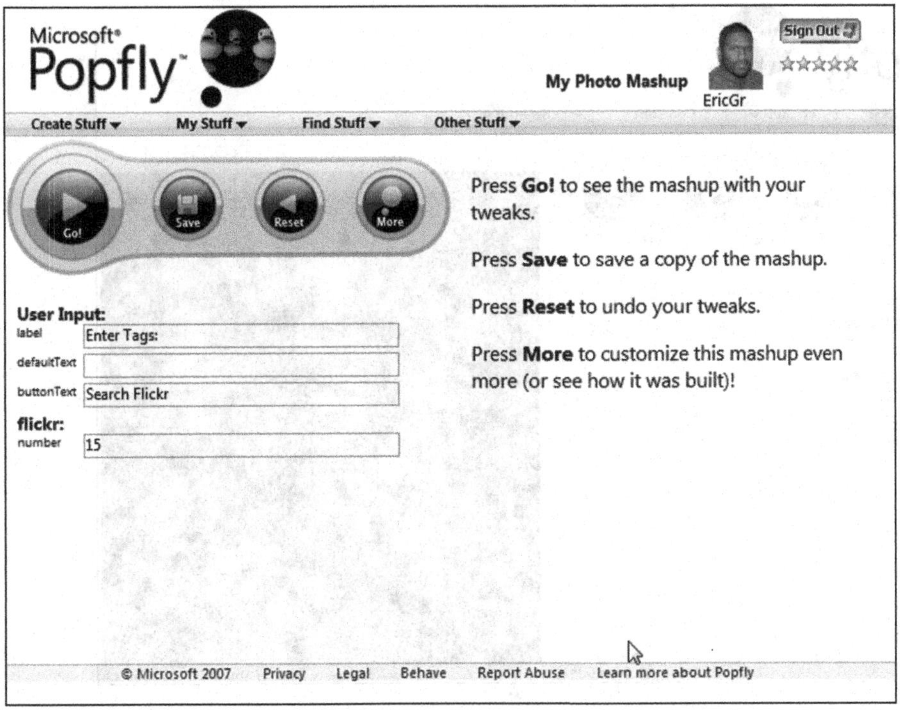

Figure 6-3. *Tweaking my photo mashup*

At the top, you have a VCR-like interface with buttons Go, Save, Reset, and More. Below the media-like interface are editable fields from the blocks contained in the mashup. Notice that you can't change the connections between blocks and how they interact. For the photo mashup, you can change the fields for two blocks: User Input and Flickr.

Remember, the Photo mashup searches Flickr's photo collection using the keywords entered in the User Input block. The User Input block has the "label", "defaultText", and "buttonText" fields available. Flickr has only the "number" field, which represents the maximum amount of photos to retrieve during the search.

Click the Go button without making any changes. Look at Figure 6-4.

Without any modifications, the mashup runs as expected. Let's make some tweaks. Change the "defaultText" to **Dogs** and the "buttonText" to **I love Dogs!**. Click the Go button to see the results of the changes, shown in Figure 6-5.

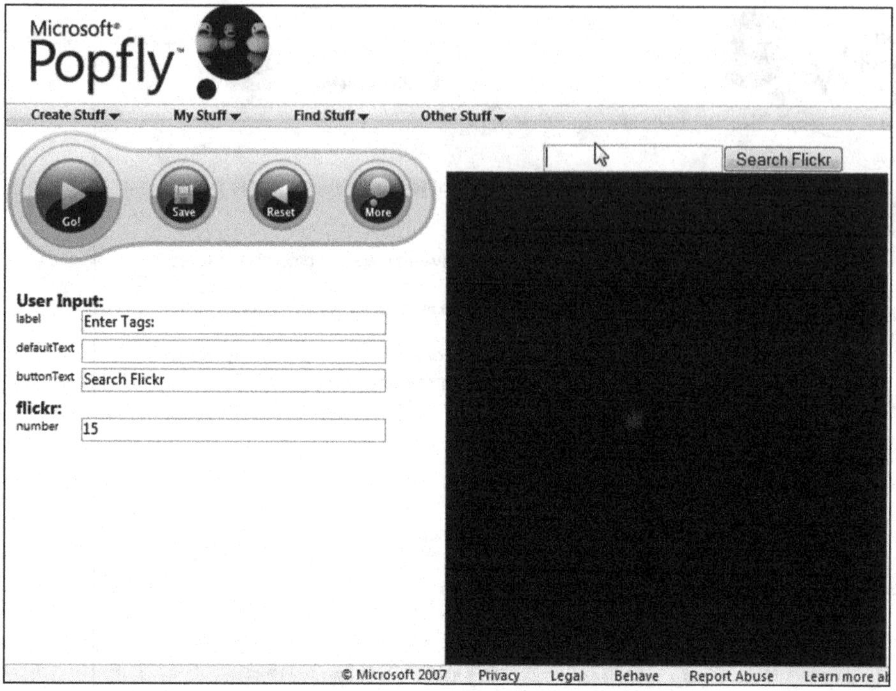

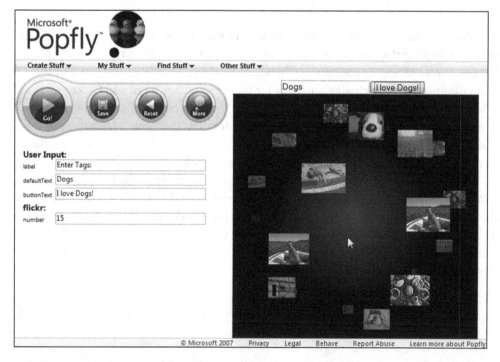

Figure 6-4. *Untweaked photo mashup*

Figure 6-5. *Tweaked my photo mashup*

If you want to make the changes permanent, click the Save button. To restore the mashup's original settings, click the Reset button. If you want to make more significant changes than Tweak It allows, click the More button to go to the mashup creator.

Sharing Your Mashup

Now that you have made tweaks to your mashup, it's time to share it! Return to the My Photo Mashup project menu by selecting My Stuff ➤ Projects from the main screen. Click the Share button (see Figure 6-6).

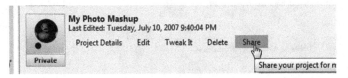

Figure 6-6. *Selecting to Share your mashup*

After clicking the Share button, the final menu option changes into the MashOut drop-down menu (see Figure 6-7). Selecting MashOut reveals the Five options are shown here for sharing your mashup:

- *Embed It*: Provides you with HTML code to paste into your custom pages

- *Download as Gadget*: Packages your mashup as a Windows Vista Gadget

- *Add to Windows Live Spaces*: Allows you to insert your mashup in your space if you have a Windows Live Space account

- *Share on Facebook*: Allows you to insert and share your mashup in Facebook if you have an account

- *Email to a Friend*: Allows you to send the mashup in an e-mail from Popfly using your Windows Live ID e-mail account

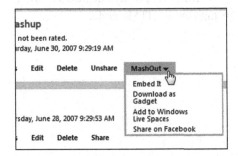

Figure 6-7. *The MashOut menu*

Sharing Your Mashup in Web Pages

Continuing to use the photo mashup as an example, let's say you have a web site, and you want to show your mashup somewhere on a custom web page you are creating. In this case, Embed It is the best option. Click MashOut ➤ Embed It to show the HTML generated by Popfly for you to use in your custom web page (see Figure 6-8).

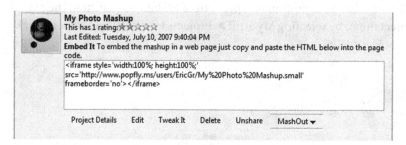

Figure 6-8. *The Embed It menu item option in action*

The generated code is an HTML IFRAME element. This block of code (see Listing 6-1) can be copied and pasted into the HTML BODY element of your web page.

Listing 6-1. *Generated IFRAME Code for Your Mashup*

```
<iframe style='width:100%; height:100%;' src='http://www.popfly.ms/users/EricGr/My➥
%20Photo%20Mashup.small' frameborder='no'></iframe>
```

Open your favorite HTML editor, which may be Notepad or a full-featured WYSIWIG (What You See Is What You Get) HTML editor like Microsoft's Expression Web (http://www.microsoft.com/expression/products/overview.aspx?key=web). I use Expression Web, so I will show it in this example. Most editors have similar functionality, so you could easily apply these instructions to another editor.

Launch Expression Web, and create a new blank web page, which will have the default name Untitled_1; see Figure 6-9. Save the page now, and name it what you like.

Select the Code viewing option at the bottom-left corner of the page editing pane to show the HTML behind the blank page. Copy the HTML from the Popfly mashup's Embed It text box, and paste it between the <body> </body> tags in the HTML code.

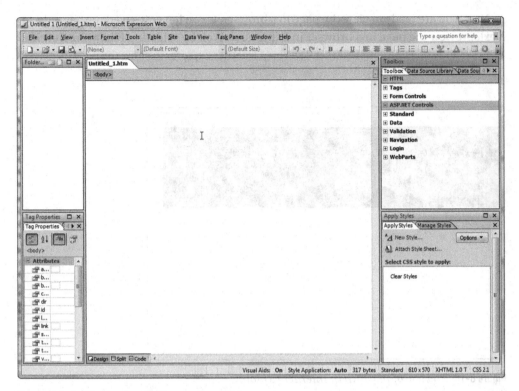

Figure 6-9. *A blank page in Expression Web*

The HTML code should look like Listing 6-2.

Listing 6-2. *Page HTML After Adding the Embed It Code*

```
<!DOCTYPE html PUBLIC "-//W3C//DTD XHTML 1.0 Transitional//EN" ➥
"http://www.w3.org/TR➥
/xhtml1/DTD/xhtml1-transitional.dtd">
<html xmlns="http://www.w3.org/1999/xhtml">

<head>
<meta http-equiv="Content-Type" content="text/html; charset=utf-8" />
<title>Untitled 1</title>
</head>

<body>
<iframe style='width:100%; height:100%;' ➥
src='http://www.popfly.ms/users/EricGr/My%➥
20Photo%20Mashup.small' frameborder='no'></iframe>
</body>

</html>
```

Now, you are ready to view the page in a browser. If you haven't saved the page, do so. Next, preview the page in a browser in Expression Web by selecting File ➤ Preview in Browser and choosing your browser. I selected Internet Explorer to show the page displayed in Figure 6-10.

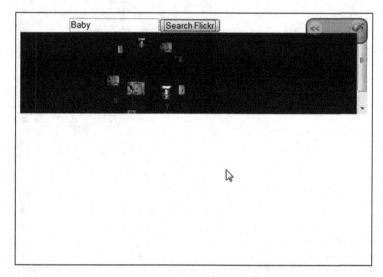

Figure 6-10. *Preview of mashup in Internet Explorer*

As you can see, the mashup appears slightly cut off and is not in the best position. A great feature of a WYSIWYG HTML editor is the ability to easily modify content with the click of a button or a drag of a mouse. Let's improve the display of the mashup. Returning to the editor and the web page, close the preview of the page, and bring the editor back to the front. In Expression Web, select the Design viewing option from the bottom of the page editing screen. You should see a graphical representation of the IFRAME you inserted. Click the IFRAME, and you should see resizing handles appear to the right of and below it (see Figure 6-11).

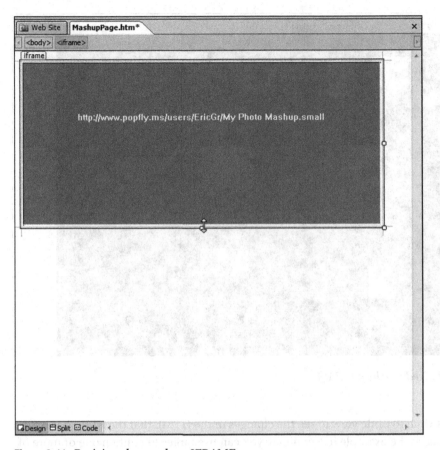

Figure 6-11. *Resizing the mashup IFRAME*

Select the bottom box (you should see the mouse arrow change to an up and down arrow); click and drag the box down to increase the size of the IFRAME; and preview the mashup again to see your changes, as shown in Figure 6-12.

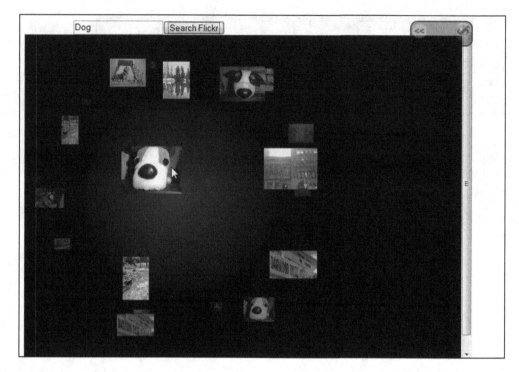

Figure 6-12. *Resized mashup IFRAME*

You can switch to Code view to see the changes in the HTML that the editor has made for you. Just as in the example in Chapter 5, you can use tables to contain one or more of your mashups. Just copy the IFRAME into the appropriate place within the TABLE tags.

Sharing Your Mashup As a Windows Vista Gadget

The Windows Sidebar is a new feature in Windows Vista that allows small applications to be docked to a transparent window on your desktop. Since mashups are usually small, visually interactive applications, your Popfly mashups are great candidates for gadgets.

■**Note** There is a complete SDK available for developing Windows Vista gadgets; to read it, go to http://msdn2.microsoft.com/en-us/library/ms723694.aspx.

Before we run through this example, make sure you have your Windows Sidebar running. To create a gadget, from the mashup project's screen, select MashOut ➤ Download as Gadget. The dialog box shown in Figure 6-13 will appear.

Figure 6-13. *The Download as Gadget mashup dialog box*

The dialog box shows the name of the gadget to be created and saved, in this case My Photo Mashup.gadget. It gives you the option to open the gadget automatically or save it to disk. I want to demonstrate a few things, so choose Save to Disk, and click the OK button. A Save As dialog box appears; choose to save with the default name, and set the location to be on your desktop.

Figure 6-14 shows the mashup on a Windows Vista desktop.

Figure 6-14. *My photo mashup saved to the desktop*

You can see that your photo mashup is recognized as a Windows Vista Gadget, because it's displayed with the default icon for gadgets.

Double-click the icon; a Windows Sidebar security dialog box is launched, asking if you want to install the gadget (see Figure 6-15).

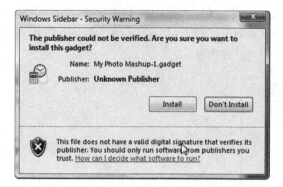

Figure 6-15. *Windows Sidebar security dialog box*

Click the Install button. After a few moments, your mashup should appear in your Windows Sidebar (see Figure 6-16). Your mashup doesn't have much screen real estate as a gadget, so if you are planning to distribute mashup gadgets, keep that in mind.

Figure 6-16. *Photo mashup in the Windows Vista Sidebar*

Each gadget has configuration options available in the upper left corner of its window. Click the gadget's wrench icon to display an About dialog box for your mashup, shown in Figure 6-17, that has two links:

- *Customize this*: This link takes you to Popfly, and if you have an account and are logged in, opens the blocks used to create the gadget in the mashup editor.

- *I want this*: This link opens the creator's Popfly page and shows the mashup information for it.

Click OK or Cancel to close the window.

You can also see your gadget along with other installed gadgets by right-clicking the Windows Sidebar and selecting the Add Gadget menu item to display a gallery of installed gadgets on your computer (see Figure 6-18).

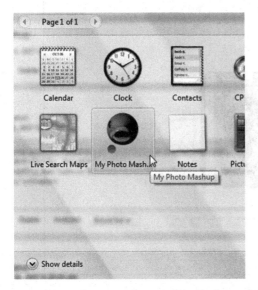

Figure 6-18. *Photo mashup gadget in the gadget gallery*

Sharing Your Mashup in Window Live Spaces

Windows Live Spaces (http://home.services.spaces.live.com/) is an online community where users can blog and share pictures and music. If you have a Windows Live Spaces account, select MashOut ➤ Add to Windows Live Spaces from the Projects page.

A new browser window opens to the Windows Live install gadget page, shown in Figure 6-19.

Click the Install button to add the mashup to your Windows Live Spaces page; Figure 6-20 shows the photo mashup in my Windows Live Spaces account. After installation, you can use Windows Live Spaces customization to move your gadget around and resize it.

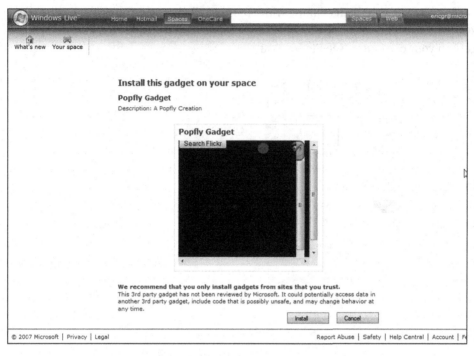

Figure 6-19. *Windows Live Spaces install gadget page*

Figure 6-20. *The photo mashup in Windows Live Spaces*

Sharing Your Mashup in Facebook

Facebook (http://www.facebook.com) is a fast-growing online community that lets users connect with others via intersecting work, school, or other social connections.

Facebook supports Popfly mashups by allowing you to post them to your profile and share them through Facebook's interface. If you have a Facebook account, go back to the Projects page, and select MashOut ➤ Share on Facebook. Facebook opens to the page shown in Figure 6-21 (if you are not logged in, you are taken to the Facebook login screen).

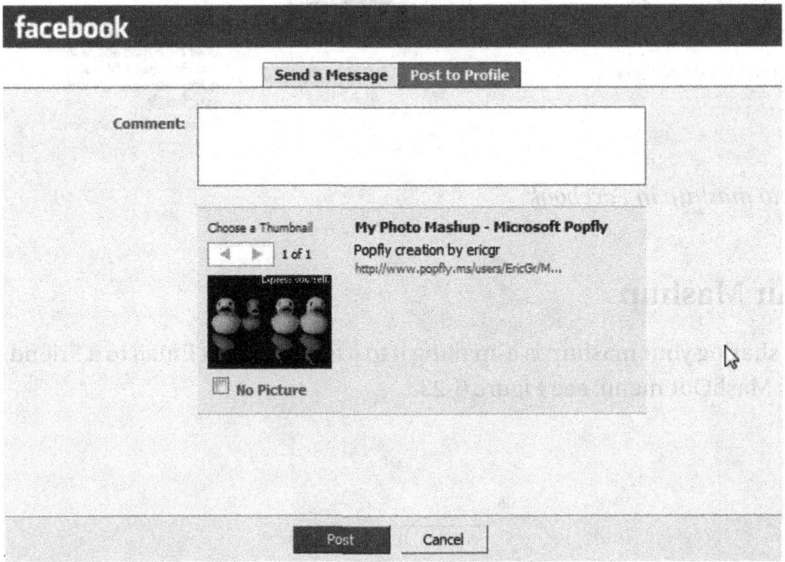

Figure 6-21. *The photo mashup Post to Profile page*

Click the Post button to complete the distribution to Facebook. Your mashup should appear in your My Posted Items section of Facebook, as shown in Figure 6-22.

Within Facebook's posted items interface, you can add comments. The Image of the mashup is the default Popfly duck image and can't be changed in Facebook.

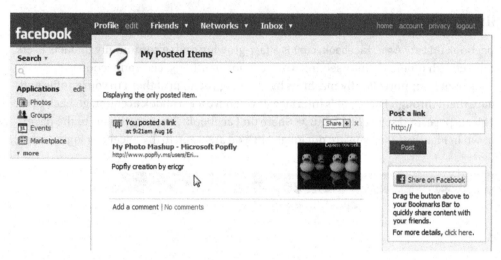

Figure 6-22. *The photo mashup in Facebook*

E-mailing Your Mashup

Another option for sharing your mashup is e-mailing it to a friend. Select Email to a Friend from the mashup's MashOut menu; see Figure 6-23.

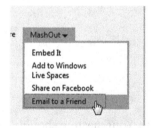

Figure 6-23. *Selecting Email to a Friend*

The window shown in Figure 6-24 opens. The Your Email field is automatically filled with your Windows Live ID, and you can type your name into the Your Name field. You type an e-mail address into the To field or log in using your Windows Live ID (by clicking the "Sign in" link on the right) to choose from a list of your contacts. The Subject field is prepopulated with, in this case, "Check out this Mashup on Microsoft Popfly: My Photo Mashup," and it is uneditable, as is the Our Stuff field. You can edit the Body field to insert your own comments before you send off your e-mail.

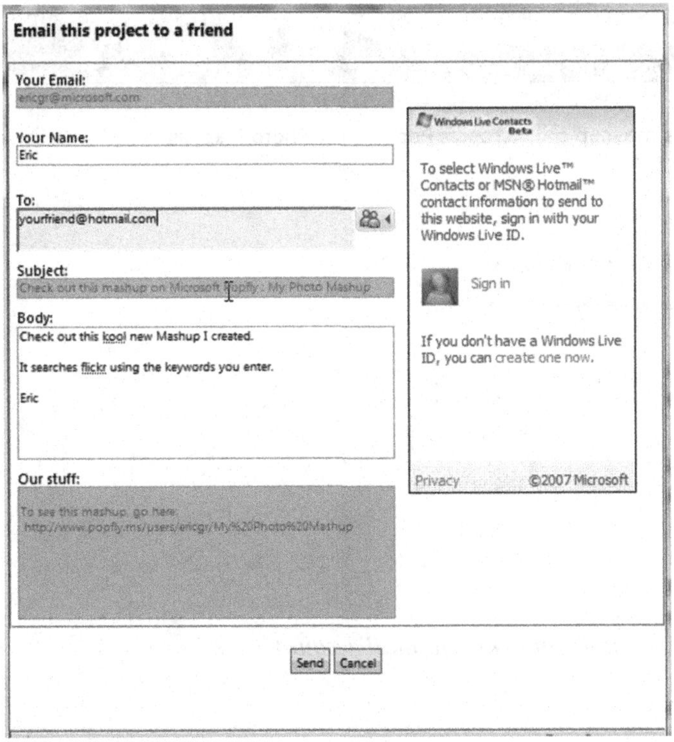

Figure 6-24. *E-mailing your mashup*

Click the Cancel button to close the window without sending the e-mail, or click Send to e-mail your friends. A window opens stating whether or not the e-mail was successfully sent (see Figure 6-25).

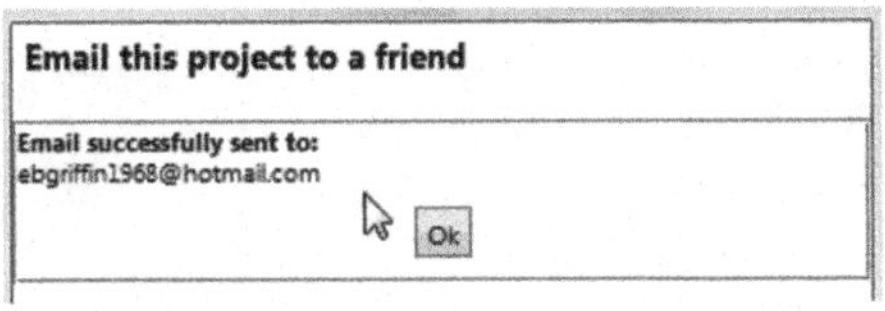

Figure 6-25. *Successful e-mail dialog box*

When recipients receive the e-mail, they are presented with the link displayed in Our Stuff. I sent the mashup to my personal Hotmail account, so I log in to Hotmail and—lo and behold—I have a message from myself (see Figure 6-26).

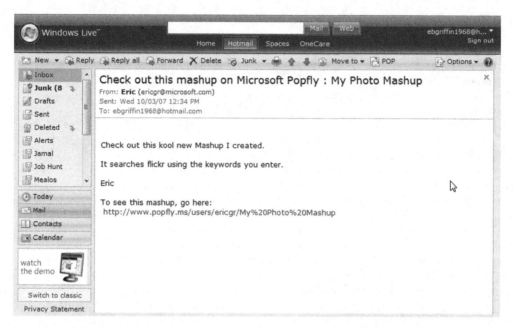

Figure 6-26. *The Popfly mashup e-mail sent to my Hotmail account*

Summary

In this chapter, I have shown you the four ways that Popfly gives to share your mashups with external users: in web pages, Windows Vista gadgets, Windows Live Spaces, and Facebook. You also learned how to e-mail your mashup. In the next chapter, you will begin examining ways to create your own reusable functionality within Popfly by creating your own Popfly blocks.

CHAPTER 7

■ ■ ■

Extending Popfly with Blocks

In Chapter 6, you explored ways you can share your mashups outside of the Popfly community. This chapter will begin examining how to create your own reusable functionality within Popfly. You can extend Popfly by the same means you have already used to create Popfly mashups: blocks. To get the most from this chapter, you will need knowledge of XML and JavaScript; I have suggested many sources of information on these in previous chapters, and I recommend you read up on them before proceeding.

What Is a Block?

A block is a packaged group of functionality; it is Popfly's way of wrapping a vendor's web service APIs or products in a way that can be easily used in Popfly mashups. Some blocks are generic to a particular technology, like the RSS block shown in Figure 7-1, which can read feeds from any blog, news source, or search engine.

Figure 7-1. *The RSS block*

Other blocks are specific to a particular service, like the MSN News Feeds block shown in Figure 7-2, which has the MSN RSS news feeds preconfigured, so you don't need to supply the URLs of each of feeds to the mashup creator.

Figure 7-2. *The MSN News Feeds block*

Block Architecture

In previous chapters, you used the mashup creator to find, drag and drop, configure, and connect blocks. You also learned how to preview, test, embed them in web pages. During all of these activities, the blocks have been executing in the Popfly Runtime Environment.

The Popfly Runtime Environment (PRE) allows you to develop and share your mashups. It requires that you define your blocks with a description and code (see Figure 7-3).

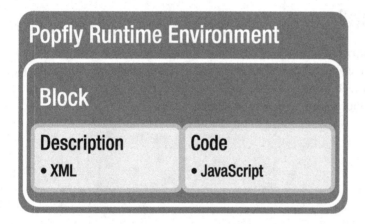

Figure 7-3. *The Popfly Runtime Environment*

The description part of the block is XML that describes the blocks properties and operations that are used by the mashup creator.

The code part of the block is the JavaScript used to execute the operations defined in the description.

Both code and description work together to provide functionality within a block. To get a better idea about how blocks are architected, let's look at the RSS block as an example (the next chapter will explain in more detail where and how to see the code for blocks).

RSS Block Description

The RSS block description is a well formed XML document that is enclosed by containing `<block class="RSSClass">` `</block>` tags (see Listing 7-1). The name of the JavaScript class created when the block is used is defined in the `class` attribute: in this case, RSSClass. Make note of this; we will come back to it later when we examine the code part of the RSS block.

■**Note** Well formed XML documents always have beginning and closing tags, for example, `<block></block>`.

Listing 7-1. *RSS Block Description*

```
<?xml version="1.0" encoding="UTF-8"?>
<block class="RSSClass">
<providerName>RSS</providerName>
  <providerUrl>http://www.popfly.ms</providerUrl>
  <providerLogoUrl>/content/components/icons/rssLogo.png</providerLogoUrl>
  <blockIconUrl>/content/components/icons/rss.png</blockIconUrl>
  <description>RSS.  Parse feeds into items that ➥
you can use in any mashup.</description>
  <suggest output="newsdisplay" input="userinput"/>
  <operations>
    <operation name="getItems" callMode="auto">
      <description>
        Retrieves items from the specified RSS feed.
      </description>
      <inputs>
        <input name="url" required="true" type="feedUrl">
          <description>The URL of the RSS feed</description>
          <defaultValue>http://blogs.msdn.com/MainFeed.aspx</defaultValue>
          <constraints/>
        </input>
      </inputs>
      <outputs>
        <output isArray="true" type="custom" object="RSSItem"/>
      </outputs>
    </operation>
    <operation name="getFeed" callMode="auto">
```

```
      <description>
        Retrieves information about the specified RSS feed.
      </description>
      <inputs>
        <input name="url" required="true" type="feedUrl">
          <description>The URL of the RSS feed</description>
          <defaultValue>http://blogs.msdn.com/MainFeed.aspx</defaultValue>
          <constraints/>
        </input>
      </inputs>
      <outputs>
        <output isArray="false" type="custom" object="RSSFeed"/>
      </outputs>
    </operation>
  </operations>
  <objects>
    <object name="RSSItem">
      <field name="title" type="title" isArray="false"/>
      <field name="link" type="url" isArray="false"/>
      <field name="description" type="description" isArray="false"/>
      <field name="source" type="string" isArray="false"/>
      <field name="sourceLink" type="url" isArray="false"/>
      <field name="author" type="name" isArray="false"/>
      <field name="tags" type="string" isArray="false"/>
      <field name="comments" type="string" isArray="false"/>
      <field name="commentRss" type="string" isArray="false"/>
      <field name="publishedDate" type="date" isArray="false"/>
      <field name="mediaLink" type="url" isArray="false"/>
      <field name="mediaType" type="string" isArray="false"/>
      <field name="latitude" type="latitude" isArray="false"/>
      field name="longtitude" type="longitude" isArray="false"/>
    </object>
    <object name="RSSFeed">
      <field name="title" type="title" isArray="false"/>
      <field name="url" type="feedUrl" isArray="false"/>
      <field name="link" type="url" isArray="false"/>
      <field name="description" type="description" isArray="false"/>
      <field name="imageURL" type="imageUrl" isArray="false"/>
    </object>
  </objects>
</block>
```

Listing 7-2 shows the block description portion of Listing 7-1 focused on the XML tags that provide basic information about the RSS block:

- `<providerName>`: The name of the block.

- `<providerUrl>`: Location of the block.

- `<providerLogoUrl>`: Location of the image that appears on the block in the mashup creator.

- `<blockIconUrl>`: Location of the image that appears in the Blocks list in the mashup creator.

- `<description>`: Text for the mashup creator describing the block and its functionality.

- `<suggest>`: Offers an output block and an input block that can be used with the block. In this case, the `newsdisplay`, or newsreader, block is suggested for the output block and the `userinput` block for input.

Listing 7-2. *Block Description XML*

```
<providerName>RSS</providerName>
<providerUrl>http://www.popfly.ms</providerUrl>
<providerLogoUrl>/content/components/icons/rssLogo.png</providerLogoUrl>
<blockIconUrl>/content/components/icons/rss.png</blockIconUrl>
<description>RSS.  Parse feeds into items that ➥
you can use in any mashup.</description>
<suggest output="newsdisplay" input="userinput"/>
```

Listing 7-3 shows the portion of the block description from Listing 7-1 focused on the XML tags for an operation for the RSS block, which you used in a previous example in Chapter 3. In particular, you used an operation that was called `getItems`.

All operations must be enclosed within an `<operation>` tag with the `name` and `callMode` attributes. The `<description>` tag is used when the block is configured in the mashup creator. The `<inputs>` tag encloses one or more `<input>` tags for each parameter used by the operation. The `<input>` tag has attributes for the name of the parameter, if it is required and the type of value it represents; also, enclosed within each `<input>` are a `<description>` tag and a `<defaultValue>` tag. Though not used by the RSS block, the `<constraints>` tag is another that you should note: use it if an operation needs to be restricted to certain inputs.

Listing 7-3. *Block Description Operation XML*

```
<operation name="getItems" callMode="auto">
  <description>
    Retrieves items from the specified RSS feed.
  </description>
  <inputs>
    <input name="url" required="true" type="feedUrl">
      <description>The URL of the RSS feed</description>
      <defaultValue>http://blogs.msdn.com/MainFeed.aspx</defaultValue>
      <constraints/>
    </input>
  </inputs>
  <outputs>
    <output isArray="true" type="custom" object="RSSItem"/>
  </outputs>
</operation>
```

If the operation has outputs, they are enclosed in the <outputs> tag, within which each output is defined with an <output> tag. If the output is an array, its type and the type of objects it contains are defined with attributes in the output tag.

As stated previously, the operation is closed with an ending </operation> tag.

Figure 7-4 shows the configuration screen of the RSS block in the mashup creator. If you refer to Figure 7-3, you can see how the XML elements match what is displayed in this configuration screen.

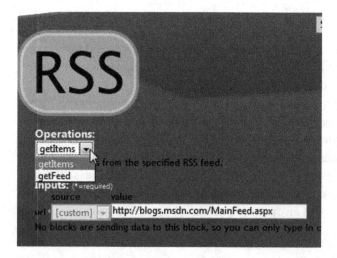

Figure 7-4. *RSS configuration screen*

All blocks have outputs. Listing 7-3 shows the portion of the block description from Listing 7-1 focused on the XML tags that define the objects used in the output of RSS. Each object used in the RSS block is contained in the <objects> tag. For the RSS block, RSSItem and RSSFeed are defined by the <object> tag with the name attribute. If you remember from Listing 7-3, the output from the getItems operation is the RSSItem object.

When a feed, in RSS XML format, is retrieved from the source, each RSS post is placed in an RSSItem object, which has fields, and each field within the object is defined in a <field> tag with name, type, and isArray attributes. Fields can contain other fields, as with the comments field in the RSSItem object. Each field in the RSSItem object corresponds to an element in an RSS XML document, so the RSSItem title field directly corresponds the RSS XML title element.

RSSItem can take the following fields:

- title: The name of the RSS post.

- link: The URL of the RSS post.

- description: The description of the post.

- source: The name of source of the post.

- sourceLink: The URL of the post's source.

- author: The name of the post's author.

- tags: Keywords for the post.

- comments: If the post allows comments, the comments will be here.

- mediaLink: The URL of any video or audio associated with the link.

- mediaType: The format of the media attached to the post (i.e. MP3, WAV).

- latitude: The associated latitude.

- longitude: The associated longitude.

Listing 7-4. *The RSSItem Object XML Definition*

```
<objects>
  <object name="RSSItem">
    <field name="title" type="title" isArray="false"/>
    <field name="link" type="url" isArray="false"/>
    <field name="description" type="description" isArray="false"/>
    <field name="source" type="string" isArray="false"/>
```

```
            <field name="sourceLink" type="url" isArray="false"/>
            <field name="author" type="name" isArray="false"/>
            <field name="tags" type="string" isArray="false"/>
            <field name="comments" type="string" isArray="false"/>
            <field name="commentRss" type="string" isArray="false"/>
            <field name="publishedDate" type="date" isArray="false"/>
    <field name="mediaLink" type="url" isArray="false"/>
            <field name="mediaType" type="string" isArray="false"/>
            <field name="latitude" type="latitude" isArray="false"/>
            <field name="longtitude" type="longitude" isArray="false"/>
            </object>
        <object name="RSSFeed">
            <field name="title" type="title" isArray="false"/>
            <field name="url" type="feedUrl" isArray="false"/>
            <field name="link" type="url" isArray="false"/>
            <field name="description" type="description" isArray="false"/>
            <field name="imageURL" type="imageUrl" isArray="false"/>
        </object>
    </objects>
```

You will notice, in Figure 7-4, the object named RSSFeed. It is used by the operation getFeed. RSSFeed represents the XML returned by the operation getFeed about the current feed used by the block.

Figure 7-5 shows the RSS block being connected to the News Reader block. After the getItems operation has been selected and configured the object that will be sent to the News Reader through the connection will be the RSSItem object.

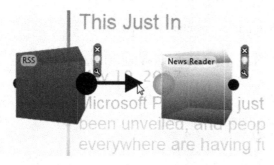

Figure 7-5. *The RSS block being connected to the News Reader block*

Once the RSS and News Reader blocks are connected, clicking the wrench icon to configure the News Reader block reveals what's shown in Figure 7-6: the source is the RSS block, and the headline, date, content, and fullStoryUrl operation input fields of the News Reader block's addNewsItem function are associated with the respective title, publishedDate, description, and link fields from the RSS block.

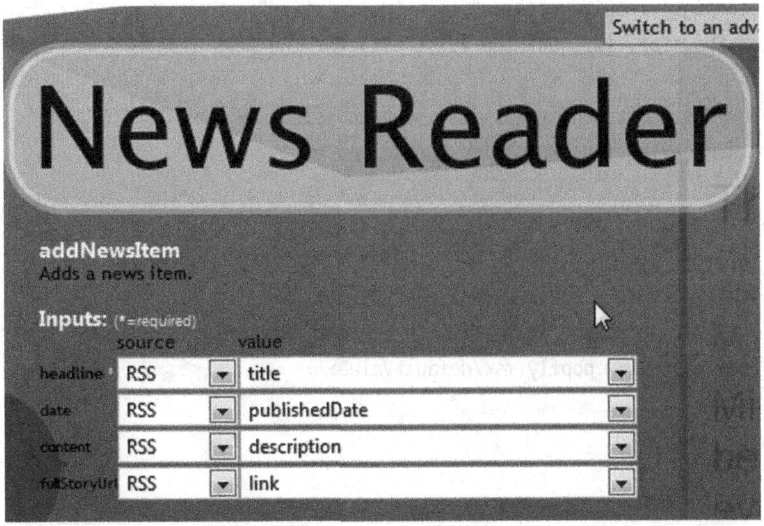

Figure 7-6. *News Reader configuration input fields*

Let's examine the addNewsItem operation definition from the News Reader block. Listing 7-5 shows a portion of the News Reader block's definition. You can see the four inputs defined within the <inputs> tag: headline, date, content, and fullStoryUrl. You can also see that the type attribute for the <input> tag is used to match the fields of an input object. In this case, the headline requires a "type" of "title", which matches the defined type RSSItem and its "title" field that are returned from the getItems RSS operation and passed to the News Reader block addNewsItem operation.

Listing 7-5. *The AddNewsItem Definition*

```
<operation name="addNewsItem">
  <description>
    Adds a news item.
  </description>
  <inputs>
    <input name="headline" required="true" type="title">
      <description>The headline for the news item.</description>
      <defaultValue>This Just In</defaultValue>
      <constraints/>
    </input>
    <input name="date" required="false" type="date">
      <description>The date of the news item.</description>
      <defaultValue>May 19, 2007</defaultValue>
      <constraints/>
    </input>
```

```
        <input name="content" required="false" type="description">
            <description>The story (or just the first bit) for the news item.➥
</description>
            <defaultValue>Microsoft Popfly has just been unveiled, ➥
and people everywhere are having fun expressing themselves!➥
</defaultValue>
            <constraints/>
        </input>
        <input name="fullStoryUrl" required="false" type="url">
            <description>A URL where the news item can be read.</description>
            <defaultValue>http://www.popfly.ms</defaultValue>
            <constraints/>
        </input>
    </inputs>
  </operation>
```

RSS Block Code

Now that we have examined how block properties and operations are defined, let's examine how they execute using JavaScript code.

The first place you saw some of the code used to execute blocks is in the advanced configuration view of the block, as shown in Figure 7-7. In the Upcoming mashup we created in Chapter 5, we used the advanced view to add code to change the map focus of the Virtual Earth control.

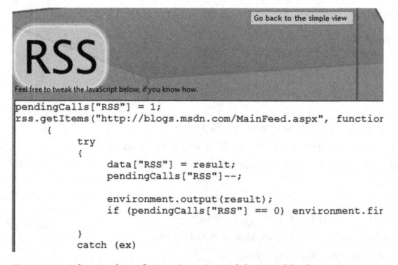

Figure 7-7. *Advanced configuration view of the RSS block*

Most of the code in this view is generated automatically by the PRE. If you type code here and later decide to return to the simple view, a dialog box will warn you that all of your added code will be lost and the block will return to the original generated code.

Looking at Listing 7-6, you should recognize the getItems operation. It is being called from the variable named rss representing the RSSClass that was defined in the <block class="RSSClass"> tag in the RSS block definition (refer to Listing 7-1).

Listing 7-6. *Advanced View Code Showing the getItems Operation*

```
pendingCalls["RSS"] = 1;
rss.getItems("http://blogs.msdn.com/MainFeed.aspx", function(result))
    {
        try
        {
            data["RSS"] = result;
            pendingCalls["RSS"]--;

            environment.output(result);
            if (pendingCalls["RSS"] == 0) environment.finish();

        }
        catch (ex)
        {
            environment.reportError(ex);
        }
    }
);
```

To get a better understanding of the RSSClass, we have to examine the entire code of the RSS block. Listing 7-7 has the JavaScript code of the RSS block.

Listing 7-7. *RSS Block JavaScript Code*

```
function RSSClass()
{
}

// Pass the requested url to base class function and get the formatted XML.
RSSClass.prototype.getFeed = function (url) {
 // Retrieves information about the specified RSS feed.
 //
```

```
// url (required): The URL of the RSS feed.
    this.__checkValidation(url);
    var returnResponse = environment.getXml(url);
    return this.__formatResponseDataRSSFeed(url, returnResponse);
};

// Pass the requested url to base class function and get the formatted XML.
RSSClass.prototype.getItems = function (url){
  // Retrieves items from the specified RSS feed.
  //
  // url (required): The URL of the RSS feed.
    this.__checkValidation(url);
    var returnResponse = environment.getXml(url);
    return this.__formatResponseDataRSSItem(returnResponse);
};

// check the validation.
RSSClass.prototype.__checkValidation  = function (url) {
    var url = this.__trimParamValue(url);

    // check for null value of URL.
    if(url.length == 0)      { throw "Please enter the URL of an RSS" }
};

// Trims white spaces from the beginning and the end of a string.
RSSClass.prototype.__trimParamValue = function (paramValue){

    if(!paramValue)
    {
        return paramValue;
    }
    else if (!isNaN(paramValue))
    {
        return paramValue;
    }

    return paramValue.trim();
};
```

```
// process the xml and create the array.
RSSClass.prototype.__formatResponseDataRSSItem = function (resultXML){
    var resultArray  = new Array();
    if(resultXML.getElementsByTagName("channel").length >= 1)
    {
        var errorCheck = resultXML.getElementsByTagName("channel")[0]➡
.getElementsByTagName("description")[0].text;
        errorLength = errorCheck.indexOf('Error');

        if(!resultXML)
        {
            throw "Sorry, the RSS block encountered a ➡
problem which it could not solve.";
        }
        if(errorLength != -1)
        {
            try
            {
                throw resultXML.getElementsByTagName("channel")[0]➡
.getElementsByTagName("description")[0].text;
            }
            catch(ex)
            {
                throw "Sorry, the RSS block encountered ➡
a problem which it could not solve.";
            }
        }
        else
        {
            var itemNodeList = resultXML.getElementsByTagName('item');
            var resultNodeCount = itemNodeList.length;
            var resultArray  = new Array(resultNodeCount);

            if(!resultNodeCount || resultNodeCount < 1)
            {
                throw "Sorry, it seems that the RSS ➡
feed does not contain any items.";
            }
```

```
            for(var i = 0; i < resultNodeCount; i++)
            {
                var itemNode = itemNodeList[i];
                if(itemNode)
                {
                    var title =           itemNode➡
.getElementsByTagName("title").length >= 1 ?  ➡
 itemNode.getElementsByTagName("title")[0].text : "";
                    var source =          itemNode➡
.getElementsByTagName("source").length>= 1 ?  ➡
     itemNode.getElementsByTagName("source")[0].text : "";
                    var sourceLink =    itemNode➡
.getElementsByTagName("source").length>= 1 ?   ➡
     itemNode.getElementsByTagName("source")[0].getAttribute("url") : "";
                    var link =            itemNode➡
.getElementsByTagName("link").length >= 1 ?➡
        itemNode.getElementsByTagName("link")[0].text : "";
                    var description =   itemNode➡
.getElementsByTagName("description").length >= 1 ?  ➡
itemNode.getElementsByTagName("description")[0].text : "";
                    var author =         itemNode➡
.getElementsByTagName("author").length >= 1 ?   ➡
    itemNode.getElementsByTagName("author")[0].text : "";
                    var tags =           itemNode➡
.getElementsByTagName("tags").length >= 1 ?   ➡
      itemNode.getElementsByTagName("tags")[0].text : "";
                    var comments =       itemNode➡
.getElementsByTagName("comments").length >= 1 ?       ➡
 itemNode.getElementsByTagName("comments")[0].text : "";
                    var commentRss =      itemNode➡
.getElementsByTagName("wfw:commentRss");

                    if(commentRss.length == 0)
                        commentRss = itemNode.getElementsByTagName("commentRss");

                    if(commentRss && commentRss.length > 0)
                        commentRss = commentRss[0].text;

                    var pubDate =        itemNode➡
.getElementsByTagName("pubDate").length >= 1 ?   ➡
   itemNode.getElementsByTagName("pubDate")[0].text : "";
                    var mediaLink =      itemNode➡
```

```
.getElementsByTagName("enclosure").length>= 1 ?        ➥
itemNode.getElementsByTagName("enclosure")[0].getAttribute("url") : "";
                var mediaType =       itemNode➥
.getElementsByTagName("enclosure").length>= 1 ? ➥
    itemNode.getElementsByTagName("enclosure")[0].getAttribute("type") : "";

                var lat =            itemNode.getElementsByTagName("geo:lat");
                var lon =            itemNode.getElementsByTagName("geo:long");

                if(lat && lat.length == 0)
                    lat = itemNode.getElementsByTagName("lat");

                if(lat && lat.length > 0)
                    lat = lat[0].text;

                if(lon && lon.length == 0)
                    lon = itemNode.getElementsByTagName("long");

                if(lon && lon.length > 0)
                    lon = lon[0].text;

                resultArray[i] = new RSSItem(title, link, description, ➥
source, sourceLink,  author, tags, comments, commentRss, pubDate,➥
mediaLink, mediaType, lat, lon);
            }
        }
        return resultArray;
    }
  }
  else
  {
      return resultArray;
  }
};

// process the xml and create the array.
RSSClass.prototype.__formatResponseDataRSSFeed = function (url, resultXML){
    if(resultXML.getElementsByTagName("channel").length >= 1)
    {
        var errorCheck = resultXML.getElementsByTagName("channel")[0]➥
.getElementsByTagName("description")[0].text;
        errorLength = errorCheck.indexOf('Error');
```

```
            if(errorLength != -1)
            {
                throw resultXML.selectSingleNode("/rss/channel/item/description").text;
            }
            else
            {
                var channelNode =   resultXML.getElementsByTagName("channel")[0];
                var title =         channelNode.getElementsByTagName("title")[0].text;
                var link =          channelNode.getElementsByTagName("link")[0].text;
                var description =   channelNode➥
.getElementsByTagName("description")[0].text;
                var imageURL;
                try
                {
                    imageURL    =       channelNode➥
.getElementsByTagName("image").length == 1 ? ➥
channelNode.getElementsByTagName("image")[0]➥
.getElementsByTagName("url")[0].text : "/content/components/icons/rss.png";
                }
                catch(ex)
                {
                    imageURL    = "##SHEL_URL##/content/components/icons/rss.png";
                }

                return new RSSFeed(title, url, link, description, imageURL);
            }
        }
        else
        {
            return new RSSFeed("", "", "", "", "");
        }
};

function RSSFeed(title, url, link, description, imageURL)
{
    this.title = title;
    this.url= url;
    this.link = link;
    this.description = description;
    this.imageURL = imageURL;
```

```
    this.toString = function() {
        return "<a href='" + environment➥
.escapeQuotes( this.url ) + "' target='_blank'>" + this.title + "</a><br>";
    };
}

function RSSItem(title, link, description, source, sourceLink, author, tags,➥
 comments, commentRss, pubDate, mediaLink, mediaType, lat, lon)
{
    this.title = title;
    this.link = link;
    this.description = description;
    this.source= source;
    this.sourceLink= sourceLink;
    this.author = author;
    this.tags= tags;
    this.comments = comments;
    this.commentRss = commentRss;
    this.publishedDate = pubDate;
    this.mediaLink = mediaLink;
    this.mediaType = mediaType;
    this.latitude = lat;
    this.longtitude = lon;
}

RSSItem.prototype.toString = function() {

    var html = "";

    html += "<strong>" + this.title + "</strong>";
    html += "<br /><font style='font-size: xx-small'>"+ this.publishedDate ➥
+"</font>" + "\n";
    html += "<p>"+ this.description +"</p><hr/>";

    return html;
};
```

All Popfly blocks require a base class to represent the functionality of the block. As stated, RSSClass is the base class for the RSS block. Listing 7-8 shows the JavaScript function that creates the RSSClass object.

Listing 7-8. *RSSClass JavaScript Function*

```
function RSSClass()
{
}
```

JavaScript object functions are defined using prototypes (though I won't go into details about JavaScript classes and prototypes here, I listed some great references in Chapter 1). If you want to create an operation for your block, you have to create a JavaScript prototype function for it. Listing 7-9 shows the prototype definition for the getItems function: url is passed into the function, and several other internal function calls are made until an array of objects of type RSSItem is returned at the end. Remember, RSS feeds are XML files.

The code that is important to note are the var returnResponse = environment. getXml(url); function, which is a helper that the PRE provides (we will talk about helper functions later in this chapter), and the return this.__formatResponseDataRSSItem(returnResponse); function, which is an internal RSS block function that takes the XML returned in the returnResponse variable and formats it into RSSItem objects. The url parameter for the environment.getXml(url); call is the same URL as the one entered in the block configuration screen: if you entered http://blogs.msdn.com/eric_griffin/rss.aspx, that would be passed as url.

Listing 7-9. *GetItems JavaScript Function Prototype*

```
// Pass the requested url to base class function and get the formatted XML.
RSSClass.prototype.getItems = function (url){
 // Retrieves items from the specified RSS feed.
 //
 // url (required): The URL of the RSS feed.
    this.__checkValidation(url);
    var returnResponse = environment.getXml(url);
    return this.__formatResponseDataRSSItem(returnResponse);
};
```

Before we examine the .__formatResponseDataRSSItem function further, let's examine Listing 7-10, which is an internal RSS block function that creates an RSSItem object from 14 parameters that make up an RSS post. This function is used by the .__formatResponseDataRSSItem function after it has parsed the XML in the returnResponse variable that was passed to it.

Listing 7-10. *RSSItem Function*

```
function RSSItem(title, link, description, source, sourceLink, author, tags, ➥
comments, commentRss, pubDate, mediaLink, mediaType, lat, lon)
{
    this.title = title;
    this.link = link;
    this.description = description;
    this.source= source;
    this.sourceLink= sourceLink;
    this.author = author;
    this.tags= tags;
    this.comments = comments;
    this.commentRss = commentRss;
    this.publishedDate = pubDate;
    this.mediaLink = mediaLink;
    this.mediaType = mediaType;
    this.latitude = lat;
    this.longtitude = lon;
}
```

Listing 7-11 shows a portion of the code of the `.__formatResponseDataRSSItem` function that parses the XML returned by the `environment.getXml(url)` call. Here, each part of the XML is searched and placed in a local variable. In this case, `itemNode`. `getElementsByTagName` is used to see if the `title` tag has anything in it and assign its value to the `title` variable. This code is used for all 14 variables that make up an RSS post.

Listing 7-11. *Parsing the RSS XML*

```
title =          itemNode.getElementsByTagName("title").length >= 1 ? ➥
        itemNode.getElementsByTagName("title")[0].text : "";var
```

After each variable is filled with the post's values, a new `RSSItem` object is created by calling the `RSSItem` function (see Listings 7-8 and 7-12), and it is added to an array. Once all of the posts have been parsed and a corresponding `RSSItem` object has been created and added to the array, the function `getItems` concludes and returns the array called `resultArray`.

Listing 7-12. *Adding a Parsed RSS XML Post to the Array*

```
                resultArray[i] = new RSSItem(title, link, description, ➥
 source, sourceLink,  author, tags, comments, commentRss, pubDate,➥
 mediaLink, mediaType, lat, lon);
```

Getting Data from the Server

Most blocks retrieve data from external sites and services. If you call a web site that resides on a domain other than Popfly, the browser's security will either prompt the user for permission or throw an error with no prompting. To prevent these situations, Popfly provides two helper functions for blocks to get data to and from any server: getXml and getText.

The getXml helper function is used to retrieve or post XML data and takes the following form: `<xmlObject> = environment.GetXml(<url>)`. It requires the following parameters:

- `<xmlObject>` is the HTTP response loaded and parsed into an XML document.

- `<url>` is the URL for which the HTTP request is to be made to, for example `http://blogs.msdn.com/eric_griffin/rss.aspx?Tags=silverlight` e.g.: `var url = "http://soapbox.msn.com/rss.aspx?searchTerm="+searchTerm; var resultXML = environment.getXml(url);`.

The getText helper method retrieves or posts text data and takes the following form: `<text> = environment.GetText(<url>)`. It accepts the following parameters:

- `<text>` is the body of the HTTP response.

- `<url >` is the URL for which the http request is to be made, for example, `http://blogs.msdn.com/eric_griffin/`.

Both getXml and getText are key functions you have to use when retrieving data from external services. If you are interested in diving deeper into how these functions work, you need to examine the code in the Popfly Block SDK, which I will be cover in the next chapter.

Summary

This chapter examined how blocks are defined with XML and executed with JavaScript. You examined the RSS and News Reader blocks from previous examples to see how the block definitions and code are used together. You learned about the Popfly Runtime Environment (PRE) and some of the helper functions it provides to make retrieving data from external sources easier. In the next chapter, we will dig deeper into creating blocks by examining the Popfly Block SDK and the tools used to build and debug blocks.

CHAPTER 8

■■■

Getting Started with the Popfly Block SDK

In Chapter 7, you learned about the architecture of Popfly blocks and how they are defined and executed with JavaScript code. In this chapter, we will begin examining the tools used to create your own reusable functionality within Popfly. You will learn what's in the SDK, how to set it up, and how it works, and I will introduce you to a helpful tool called Visual Web Developer.

Downloading the Popfly Block SDK

The Popfly team has created a software development kit (SDK) for blocks. You can get the SDK from the Popfly site's block creation area, accessible by clicking Create Stuff ➤ Block; see Figure 8-1.

Figure 8-1. *The block creator*

If the Tutorial window shown in Figure 8-2 is not visible, you can open it by clicking on the double left-facing arrow (<<) icon;

Figure 8-2. *Tutorial Window*

Click the "block building guide" link in the Tutorial window (http://www.popfly.ms/ Help/PopflyBlockSDK.zip) to open a save dialog box for you to save the SDK, which is in the zipped filed called PopflyBlockSDK.zip. If you are using Firefox, you will see the dialog box shown in Figure 8-3. Internet Explorer's dialog box is similar. Click Save to Disk, and choose a location (like the desktop) for the file download.

Figure 8-3. *Firefox's save dialog box*

After completing the download, unzip the contents into a folder. Remember to save the file contents with folder names extraction option to make sure you preserve the directory structure of the folders in the SDK.

Go to the location where you unzipped the SDK, and you should see the root directory structure shown in Figure 8-4.

Figure 8-4. *The Block SDK root directory structure*

The Tester directory holds the development examples and the block test harness (more on the test harness later). BlockSchema.xsd is an XML document used to validate the XML structure of blocks. If you recall from Chapter 7, XML documents are used to describe a block's operations and properties.

The Adobe PDF document called Building Blocks.pdf is the documentation of the SDK. It has a brief overview of the block creation process. The Types.xsd document is another XML schema document; it's used to validate the types of objects that can be described in a block's operations and properties, for example, URL, string, decimal, and so on.

Note If you want to know more about schemas, a great place to start is Wikipedia's article at http:// en.wikipedia.org/wiki/XML_schema.

Navigate into the Tester folder to see the directory structure shown in Figure 8-5. This folder is where the main development of blocks occurs, and it's the root directory of the block test harness. The test harness is a way for you to develop Popfly blocks without accessing the entire Popfly environment or even having to be online.

The technological base for the SDK is Microsoft's .NET, so many of the items in the SDK are specific to .NET development; you can find out general information about .NET at http://msdn2.microsoft.com/netframework/default.aspx.

The bin, obj, and properties folders are used by the .NET test harness and the tools that we will be talking about later. You will notice six other files in the root directory that are used by the test harness: Default.aspx, Default.aspx.cs, Default.aspx.designer.cs,

Tester.sln, Tester.csproj, and Web.config. These files are used by the tool that I will introduce in the next section.

Figure 8-5. *Tester root directory*

Installing Visual Web Developer

The files in Tester.csproj are the files that make up the test harness. They are written in .NET and require a .NET development environment to execute. The Popfly team recommends the Microsoft Visual Studio development environment, in particular a version called Microsoft Visual Web Developer Express 2005—and it is absolutely free to download, install, and use.

■Note At the time of this writing, Visual Web Developer 2005 was the recommended development tool for Popfly blocks. The 2008 version of Visual Web Developer should be available at the time of this book's publication, but the instructions in this chapter and future chapters should change very little.

You can download Visual Web Developer by going to http://msdn2.microsoft.com/express/aa975050.aspx. Select a language for Visual Web Developer, and a download dialog box will appear (see Figure 8-6). Choose a download location for the installation executable called vwdsetup.exe.

Navigate to the location where you downloaded vwdsetup.exe, and double-click it to begin the installation. Click through the installation (choose the default options), which will download additional files (see Figure 8-7). You also have the option to download the MSDN library help files. I recommend you do this so you can have further reference material about .NET and Visual Web Developer.

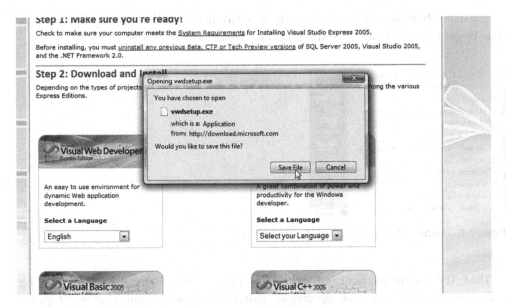

Step 1: Make sure you're ready!

Check to make sure your computer meets the System Requirements for Installing Visual Studio Express 2005.

Before installing, you must uninstall any previous Beta, CTP or Tech Preview versions of SQL Server 2005, Visual Studio 2005, and the .NET Framework 2.0.

Step 2: Download and Install

Depending on the types of projects .... ong the various Express Editions.

Opening vwdsetup.exe

You have chosen to open

⬜ **vwdsetup.exe**

    which is a: Application

    from: http://download.microsoft.com

Would you like to save this file?

[Save File]   [Cancel]

An easy to use environment for dynamic Web application development.

Select a Language

[English ▾]

A great combination of power and productivity for the Windows developer.

Select a Language

[Select your Language ▾]

Visual Basic 2005

Visual C++ 2005

Figure 8-6. *The Visual Web Developer download page*

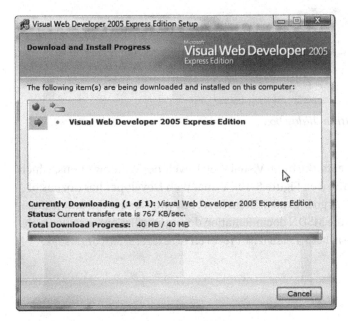

Figure 8-7. *Visual Web Developer installation*

The dialog box will indicate a successful installation. You can launch Visual Web Developer by going to the Windows Start menu and clicking its icon (see Figure 8-8).

Figure 8-8. *Starting Microsoft Visual Web Developer*

The first thing that happens is that the dialog box shown in Figure 8-9 appears, stating that Visual Web Developer is configuring itself for the first time (this dialog box won't appear again).

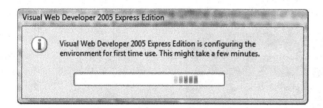

Figure 8-9. *First time configuration dialog box*

After the dialog box disappears, the main Visual Web Developer Window opens, which has several menus and windows (see Figure 8-10). Visual Web Developer has dozens of features and capabilities. I won't go into all of them here, but you can use the online documentation (if you downloaded the MSDN documentation during installation) or return to the Visual Web Developer web site at http://msdn2.microsoft.com/express/aa700797.aspx.

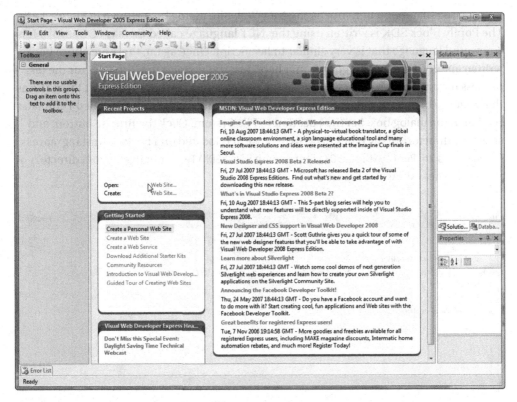

Figure 8-10. *The main window of Visual Web Developer*

Setting Up the Block Test Harness

What you are going to do next is get the Popfly SDK block test harness up and running within Visual Web Developer (VWD). In order to do that, we have to create a new web site project in VWD.

Select File ➤ New Web Site (see Figure 8-11).

Figure 8-11. *Selecting New Web Site*

Selecting that menu item opens the New Web Site dialog box (shown in Figure 8-12).
The Popfly Block SDK is written using the .NET language called C# (say "C Sharp"). It is
a powerful language that is very similar to JavaScript. Once again, there are entire books
written about C#, so I won't go into that here. Just understand that, in order for the test
harness to run properly, the language of the project must be set to C#. Select Visual C# as
the language of the site. Select Empty Web Site from the Visual Studio Installed Templates
section of the dialog box. Set the Location to File System. Click the Browse button, and
select the directory of the block SDK. In my case, it is located on I:\Book Writing\Apress\
Foundations of Popfly\BlockSDK\Tester with BlockSDK\Tester being the root directory of
the test harness shown in Figure 8-12.

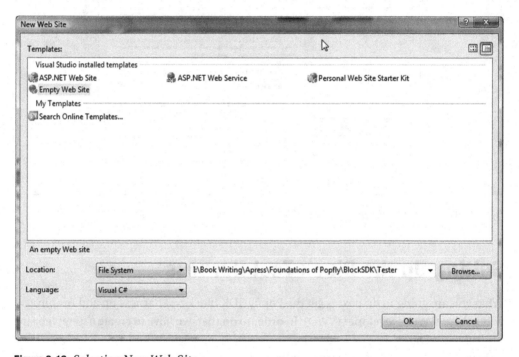

Figure 8-12. *Selecting New Web Site*

Click the OK button, and the Web Site Already Exists dialog box should appear (see
Figure 8-13). By default, the "Select a new folder to create your Web site" option is selected.
We don't want to do this, because it will create a new folder underneath the root folder
(i.e., BlockSDK\Tester\Tester). Select "Open the existing Web site", because we want to
use the Tester root folder as our web site.

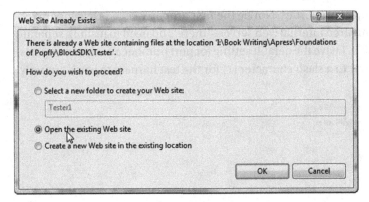

Figure 8-13. *Selecting "Open the existing Web site"*

After pressing the OK button, you will be returned to the VWD main window. To the upper left is a window with Solution Explorer tab that represents the web site you just created (see Figure 8-14). The Solution Explorer is a tree list that works like a virtual disk drive showing you all of the files and folders that the project uses. You should see all of the folders and many of the files that you saw in the root Tester folder in Figure 8-14. A couple of files are hidden, but we will go into that later.

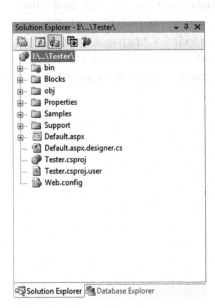

Figure 8-14. *Visual Web Developer's Solution Explorer*

Select the project at the top of the list to select the project. Below the Solution Explorer is the Properties window (see Figure 8-15). As you select folders and objects in the Solution Explorer, the folder or objects properties show in this window. With the project selected, you can see the Tester project properties. Notice the first property called Developer Web Server. VWD has a preconfigured internal web server—there's no need to install a separate web server to do your testing. Leave the default setting for port number and dynamic ports. Set the virtual path property to a slash character (/) for the test harness to work properly.

Figure 8-15. *Tester project settings*

Now that we have the project set up, let's start the block test harness. First, make sure the test harness's default page starts up in the web browser by right-clicking Default.aspx (see Figure 8-16) and selecting Set As Start Page. Similar to index.htm pages, default.aspx pages are .NET pages that are started up by web sites when you navigate to a URL. Since you are using a development tool, though, you have complete control over what is started first by the internal web server.

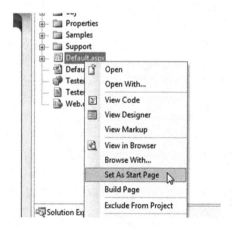

Figure 8-16. *Selecting Set As Start Page*

Once that is completed, we want to start debugging the project. That can be accomplished by selecting the Debug ➤ Start Debugging menu item or clicking the Start Debugging button, as shown in Figure 8-17.

Figure 8-17. *Starting the debugging process*

A browser window should open, with the test harness running (see Figure 8-18). The URL for my web site is `http://localhost:56488/Tester/Default.aspx`. So VWD started its internal web server localhost set to port 56488 (remember the settings in Figure 8-15) to the web site Tester and opened the default page set to `Default.aspx`.

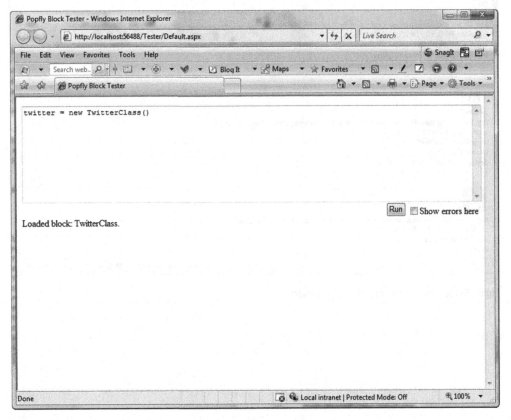

Figure 8-18. *Visual Web Developer running the block test harness*

The test harness is bare bones and nothing fancy. It has a text box at the top, a Run button, and an option box labeled "Show errors here". Before we dig into the details, let's make something happen. Below the text `twitter = new TwitterClass()` type **twitter. getLatestPosts()**.

Click the Run button, and after a few moments, content should appear below the text box, as shown in Figure 8-19.

Figure 8-19. *Test harness showing results*

You've just successfully run the test harness. The harness will be a central place for you to test your blocks. But now, it's time for you to further understand how the harness works and how to configure it to work with your blocks.

How the Test Harness Works

Before we go into the how things work, stop the currently running test harness by selecting Debug ➤ Stop Debugging or clicking the Stop Debugging button in the VWD window (see Figure 8-20).

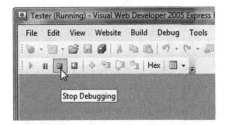

Figure 8-20. *Clicking Stop Debugging*

Returning to VWD, go to the Solution Explorer. The block test harness works with files that are located in the Blocks directory. If you want to test your new block creation, you have to put it in here. Select or expand the Blocks directory in the Solution Explorer window. You should see three files in the Blocks folder: We are interested in is the Twitter.js file (at the time of this writing in October 2007, the other two files are not complete and are not useful, so I won't cover them here). The .js file extension is recognized by Visual Web Developer as a JavaScript file—remember, block code is JavaScript. Also, if you recall, when we ran the test harness, we were typing JavaScript and referencing an object called TwitterClass.

Twitter is a social networking and microblogging service utilizing instant messaging, SMS, or a web interface. Therefore, the code in Twitter.js is JavaScript code that accesses a Twitter repository and prints out the results.

Let's go look at the code by double-clicking the Twitter.js file in Solution Explorer (see Figure 8-21).

Figure 8-21. *Double-clicking Twitter.js*

The code for `Twitter.js` will open in the VWD editor. To create more room to examine the code, click the Autohide icon in the Toolbox window. Note that all windows in VWD have this capability (see Figure 8-22).

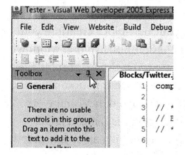

Figure 8-22. *Autohiding windows*

VWD has a rich editor that has first-class capabilities. It recognizes JavaScript keywords and color codes them for easier identification and reading. There are many more features in the developer that you can read about in the documentation.

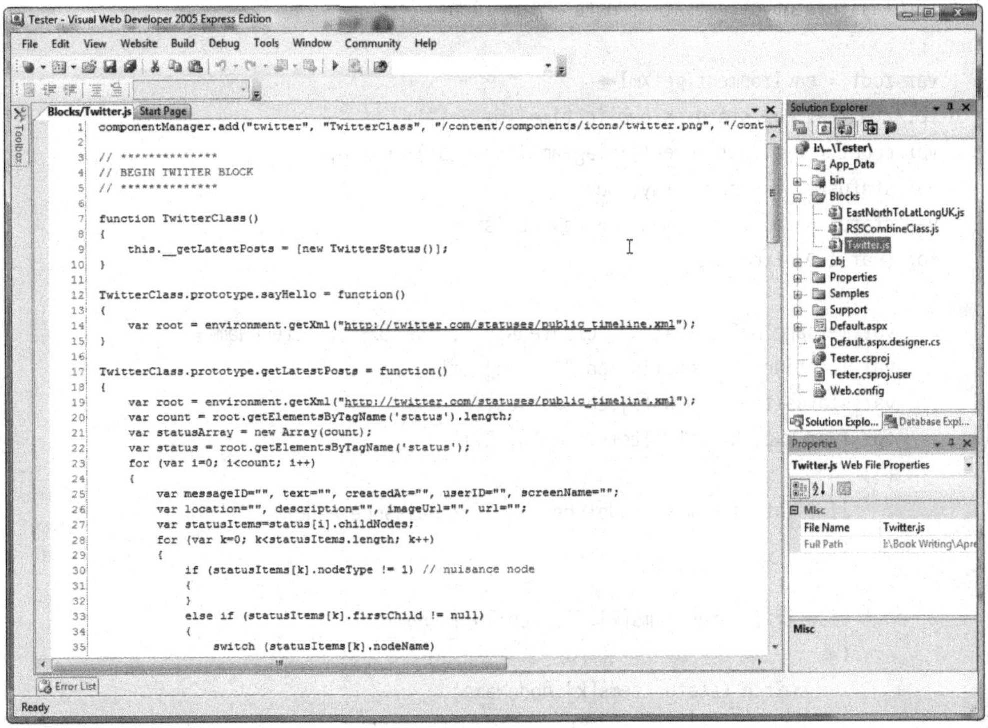

Figure 8-23. *Twitter.js in the VWD editor*

If you need to refresh your memory about how blocks are structured, refer to Chapter 7. The Twitter.js code is shown in Listing 8-1 for your reference.

Listing 8-1. *Twitter Block Source Code*

```
componentManager.add("twitter", "TwitterClass", ➥
"/content/components/icons/twitter.png",
"/content/components/icons/twitterLogo.png");


// *************
// BEGIN TWITTER BLOCK
// *************


function TwitterClass()
{
    this.__getLatestPosts = [new TwitterStatus()];
}
```

```
TwitterClass.prototype.getLatestPosts = function()
{
    var root = environment.getXml➥
("http://twitter.com/statuses/public_timeline.xml");
    var count = root.getElementsByTagName('status').length;
    var statusArray = new Array(count);
    var status = root.getElementsByTagName('status');
    for (var i=0; i<count; i++)
    {
        var messageID="", text="", createdAt="", userID="", screenName="";
        var location="", description="", imageUrl="", url="";
        var statusItems=status[i].childNodes;
        for (var k=0; k<statusItems.length; k++)
        {
            if (statusItems[k].nodeType != 1) // nuisance node
            {
            }
            else if (statusItems[k].firstChild != null)
            {
                switch (statusItems[k].nodeName)
                {
                    case "id" :
                    {
                        messageID = statusItems[k].firstChild.nodeValue;
                        break;
                    }
                    case "text" :
                    {
                        text = statusItems[k].firstChild.nodeValue;
                        break;
                    }
                    case "created_at" :
                    {
                        createdAt = statusItems[k].firstChild.nodeValue;
                        break;
                    }
                    case "user" :
                    {
                        var userItems = statusItems[k].childNodes;
                        for (var l=0;l<userItems.length;l++)
                        {
```

```
                    if (userItems[1].nodeType != 1)
                    {
                    }
                    else if (userItems[1].firstChild != null)
                    {
                        switch (userItems[1].nodeName)
                        {
                            case "id" :
                            {
                                userID = userItems[1].firstChild.nodeValue;
                                break;
                            }
                            case "screen_name" :
                            {
                                screenName = userItems[1]➥
.firstChild.nodeValue;

                                break;
                            }
                            case "location" :
                            {
                                location = userItems[1]➥
.firstChild.nodeValue;

                                break;
                            }
                            case "description" :
                            {
                                description = userItems[1]➥
.firstChild.nodeValue;

                                break;
                            }
                            case "profile_image_url" :
                            {
                                imageUrl = userItems[1]➥
.firstChild.nodeValue;
                                // HACK: twitter sometimes➥
 return url as blah.comsystem/blah
                                // instead of blah.com/system/blah
                                imageUrl = imageUrl➥
.replace("comsystem", "com/system");
                                break;
                            }
```

```
                                case "url" :
                                {
                                    url = userItems[1].firstChild.nodeValue;
                                    break;
                                }
                            } //inner switch
                        } //inner else if switch
                    } //inner for
                }// case
            }//switch
        }//outer else if
    }//for (k)
    statusArray[i] = new TwitterStatus(messageID, text,➥
 createdAt, userID, screenName,➥
location, description,imageUrl, url);
    } //for (i)
    return statusArray;
}


function TwitterStatus(messageID, text, createdAt, userID, screenName, ➥
 location, description, imageUrl, url)
{
    this.messageID = messageID;
    this.text = text;
    this.createdAt = createdAt;
    this.userID = userID;
    this.screenName = screenName;
    this.location = location;
    this.description = description;
    this.imageUrl = imageUrl;
    this.url = url;
    this.toString = function()
    {
        var sb = new Sys.StringBuilder();
        sb.append("<img border='0' src='" + this.imageUrl + "' >" + "<br>");
        sb.append("text: " + this.text + "<br>");
        sb.append("createdAt: " + this.createdAt + "<br>");
        sb.append("screenName: " + this.screenName + "<br>");
        sb.append("location: " + this.location + "<br>");
        sb.append("description: " + this.description + "<br>");
        sb.append("<a href='" + this.url + "'>link</a>" + "<br>");
```

```
        sb.append("<p/>");
        return sb.toString();
    }
}
// *************
// END TWITTER BLOCK
// *************
```

The first line of code is the most important in relation to using the block test harness to test your blocks. A call is made to an object called componentManager:

```
componentManager.add("twitter", "TwitterClass", ➡
"/content/components/icons/twitter.png",➡
"/content/components/icons/twitterLogo.png");
```

An add method is called with four parameters. The first two are the most important parameters; the last two refer to images that represent the block and are not required for the block to run in the harness.

The first parameter, twitter, is the name of the variable that will hold the object created in the second parameter. TwitterClass is the object representing the block and is passed into the second parameter. The function TwitterClass is created to represent the block (from Listing 8-1).

```
function TwitterClass()
{
    this.__getLatestPosts = [new TwitterStatus()];
}
```

The SDK object componentManager uses these parameters to load the block into the test harness. You can see if your block has been loaded by looking below the text box when the test harness is running (see Figure 8-24).

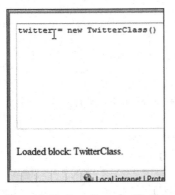

Figure 8-24. *Loading the TwitterClass block*

Looking further into Listing 8-1, you can find familiar utility objects, detailed in Chapter 7. The environment object is used in the getLatestPosts() function to retrieve the XML generated by the Twitter service and referenced by the URL http://twitter.com/statuses/public_timeline.xml:

```
var root = environment➡
.getXml("http://twitter.com/statuses/public_timeline.xml");
```

From there, the JavaScript code of the function parses the XML in the root variable to retrieve the Twitter data and assigns the data to a corresponding variable: messageID, text, createdAt, userID, screenName, location, description, imageUrl, or url:

```
statusArray[i] = new ➡
TwitterStatus(messageID, text, createdAt, userID, screenName,➡
location, description,imageUrl, url);
```

Similar to the RSS object we examined in Chapter 7, the objects are created using the variables and the function TwitterStatus() (see Listing 8-2) and assigned into an array.

Listing 8-2. *TwitterStatus Function*

```
function TwitterStatus(messageID, text, createdAt, userID, screenName, ➡
 location, description, imageUrl, url)
{
    this.messageID = messageID;
    this.text = text;
    this.createdAt = createdAt;
    this.userID = userID;
    this.screenName = screenName;
    this.location = location;
    this.description = description;
    this.imageUrl = imageUrl;
    this.url = url;

 this.toString = function()
    {
        var sb = new Sys.StringBuilder();
        sb.append("<img border='0' src='" + this.imageUrl + "' >" + "<br>");
        sb.append("text: " + this.text + "<br>");
        sb.append("createdAt: " + this.createdAt + "<br>");
        sb.append("screenName: " + this.screenName + "<br>");
        sb.append("location: " + this.location + "<br>");
        sb.append("description: " + this.description + "<br>");
```

```
        sb.append("<a href='" + this.url + "'>link</a>" + "<br>");
        sb.append("<p/>");
        return sb.toString();
    }
}
```

Each object has a special function called `toString` that is created to transform the data into HTML that is used by the test harness when the results are returned (see Figure 8-19).

If you are really interested in the code that creates the test harness and the code used to emulate the Popfly objects, like the `componentManager` (`componentManager.js`) and the `environment` (`environment.js`) object, look in the `Support` folder in Solution Explorer and double-click the files you are interested in (see Figure 8-25). Notice that the full Microsoft JavaScript Ajax Library is available to Popfly blocks. You can learn more about the rich capabilities of this library at Microsoft's Ajax site at `http://asp.net/ajax/`.

Remember that `.aspx`, and `.cs` files are .NET-specific technologies and are beyond the scope of this book.

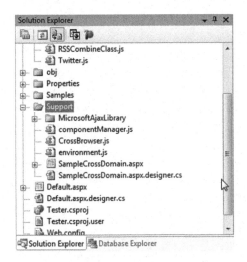

Figure 8-25. *Support folder files*

Summary

In this chapter, we have examined the Popfly Block SDK. You have learned that the Popfly SDK has a test harness created with .NET technology, and it can be run in a free tool from Microsoft called Visual Web Developer. In the next chapter, you will use Visual Web Developer to create and debug your own blocks.

CHAPTER 9

■ ■ ■

Creating Your First Block with Visual Web Developer

In Chapter 8, you learned about the Popfly SDK and how to use Microsoft Visual Web Developer to run it. In this chapter, you will walk through the creation of a block from scratch using the SDK and Visual Web Developer (VWD). We will also briefly explore the debugging capabilities of VWD and how it can help you test your block code.

Finding a Service for Your Block

The first thing you need to do is decide what functionality you want in your block. You can decide to create self-contained functionality that doesn't depend on external services, but what fun would that be? The value proposition of mashups is the mixing of different services from different vendors, so it's best to look around a site that you use and see if they have an API that can be programmed into a block.

For my example, I decided to create a Technorati block. This block will use the API published by Technorati. Technorati is a search engine that specializes in blogs. You can check it out by going to http://www.technorati.com. A screenshot of its home page can be seen in Figure 9-1.

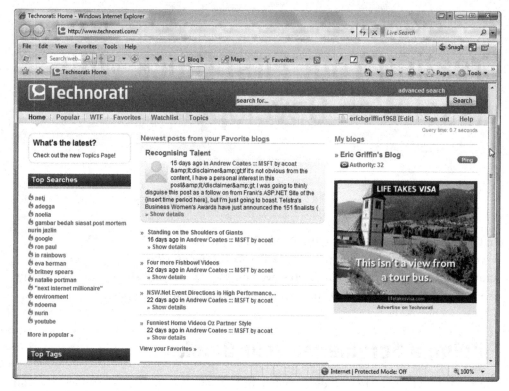

Figure 9-1. *Technorati's home page*

I use Technorati all the time to search blogs and dig into a particular topic. Technorati is more than a search engine; there are many other features that make it an invaluable tool for bloggers and researchers. After navigating your browser to Technorati's home page, type **Silverlight** into the search box at the top of the window to see a result similar to Figure 9-2.

Not only are you given results from hundreds of blogs based on your search words, you are given a credibility rating for the blogs' authors. The rating is based on the number of people who link back to the post as a source, so the more people who link to your post, the higher the rating goes—cool. Technorati also provides an API for registered users to use for their own purposes.

Before you can use the API, you need to become a registered user. From the Technorati page, click the Join link to start the registration process (see Figure 9-3).

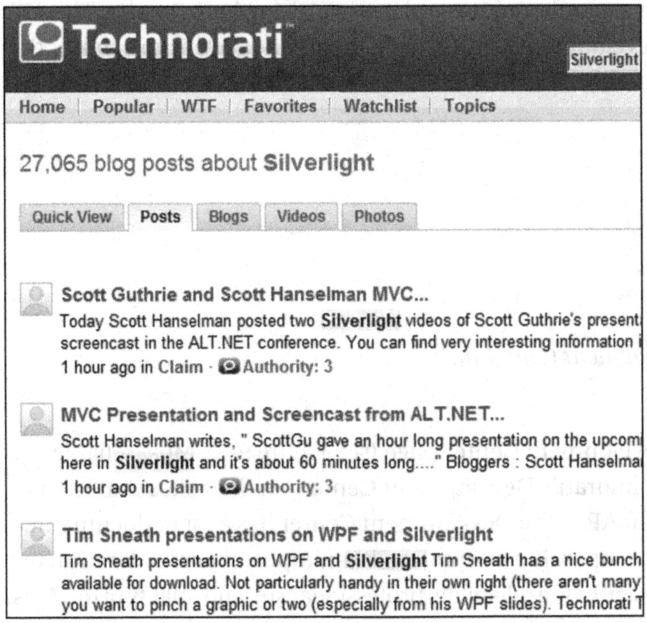

Figure 9-2. *Technorati search results*

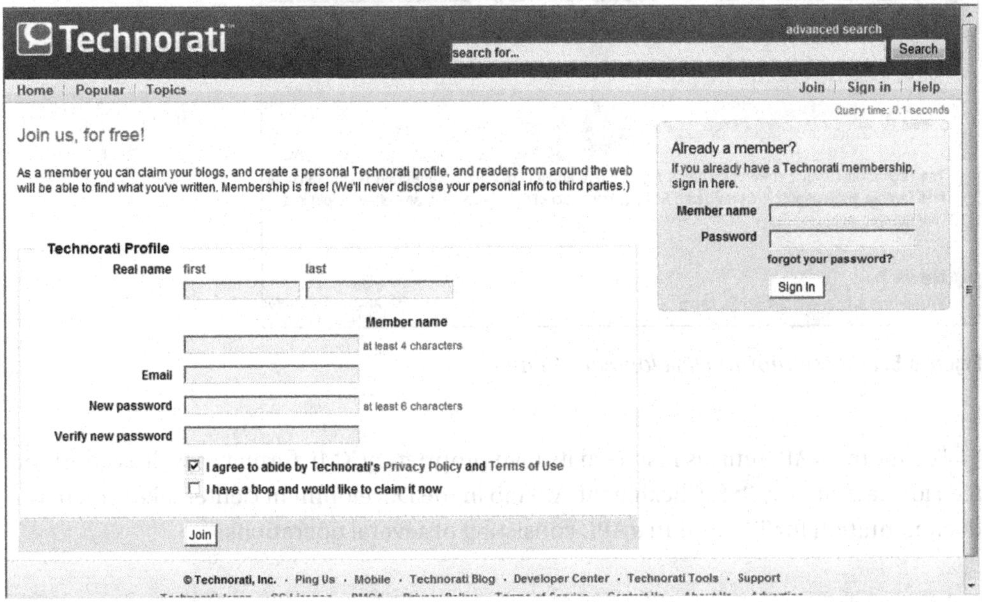

Figure 9-3. *Technorati's registration screen*

Once you are registered with a member name and password, log in to the site. The API information is located in the Development Center, which you can reach from a link at the bottom of the page (see Figure 9-4).

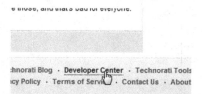

Figure 9-4. *The Technorati Development Center link*

Click the link to go to the Development Center page (see Figure 9-5). Most reliable providers have an area, like Technorati's Development Center, on their sites that is for developers who want to use their APIs; the Development Center has a lot of documentation and tutorials. Extensive developer documentation is an important consideration on the service you want to use. It is a sign of the reliability, professionalism, and quality of the APIs.

Figure 9-5. *The Technorati Development Center*

Technorati's API returns results in its own proprietary XML format as well as common feed formats such as RSS. Clicking the API tab in the Development Center takes you to the documentation for Technorati's API, consisting of several operations.

Note Each vendor has its own terminology for API operations. Technorati decided to call their operations "queries." We are going to use "operations" to remain consistent with Popfly block terminology.

Technorati API Operations

Technorati documentation states that the API has eight operations that you can use in your programming adventures. They are categorized as Search, Browsing, Blog Information, and Member Information.

Search

The Search category contains the following operations:

- cosmos: Provides blogs that link to a given URL

- search: Allows you to searching posts using a keyword or phrase

- tag: Allows you to searching posts that are tagged with a specific topic

- dailycounts: Provides a count of posts containing the queried keywords

Browse

The Browse category contains the following operation:

- toptags: Provides the most frequently searched indexed tags by Technorati

Blog Information

The Blog Information category contains the following operations:

- bloginfo: Links the count, rank, and available feed information about a specific blog URL

- blogposttags: Provides the top tags used by a specific blog

Member Information

The Member Information category contains the following operations:

- getinfo: Provides Technorati member information like full name of an author and other blogs by the same author

There is certainly a lot to choose from, but you have to keep in mind how it might be used as a block. You can certainly choose to expose all of the APIs of a given service, in this case, all eight operations. To stay more focused on creating blocks, we are going to use one operation—search. After I walk you through exposing this operation in the block, you can go back and add the remaining operations if you like. This approach is generally good when you are developing new blocks: it takes you through the entire process and then allows you to build incrementally.

So let's read a little more about the Technorati search operation.

Search Operation (Query)

The search operation is a keyword search that lets you see which blogs contain a given search string. This operation is the same as the search we did on the Technorati site when we typed the keyword "Silverlight" in the search box to return a list of blogs containing that term. The API version allows more features and gives you a way to use the search function on your own site.

The query is made using a RESTful interface (refer to the discussion of this technology in Chapter 1 for more information). To make a query, you need to send either an HTTP GET or an HTTP POST request to http://api.technorati.com/search?key=[apikey]&query=[words] with the mandatory parameters key and query and the additional optional parameters described in the following section.

Mandatory Parameters

These are the mandatory parameters for the search query.

- key: Use this to specify your Technorati API key.

- query: Set this to the words you are searching for. Separate words with a plus sign (+) as usual.

Optional Parameters

You may also want to include the following optional parameters when creating the search query:

- format: This allows you to request an output format, which by default is set to xml. At the moment, only the XML (xml) and RSS (rss) formats are supported. There are plans to support the Atom syndication format, as well as XOXO in the near future.

- language: Set this to an ISO 639-1 two-character language code to retrieve results specific to that language. This feature is currently in its beta phase and may not work for all languages.

- authority: Set this to filter results to those from blogs with at least the Technorati Authority that you specify. Technorati calculates a blog's authority by how many people link to it. Filtering by authority is a good way to refine your search results. There are four settings:

  - n: These results may have any authority, so all results are returned.

  - a1: Results at this setting have a little authority; blogs have at least one link.

  - a4: This setting returns blogs with some authority; results contain blogs with a handful of links.

  - a7: This setting returns only blogs with a lot of authority, that is, with hundreds of links.

- start: Set this to a number larger than 0, and you'll get the 20 (start+20) freshest items (links or blogs); set it to 20+1, and you'll get the second page of rankings, that is, items 21–40.

- limit: Set this to a number larger than 0 and smaller or equal to 100, and it will return limit number of links for a query. By default, this value is 20.

- claim: Set this to 1 to have each link result embellished with any user information associated with a link result's parent blog.

Examining the operation, we see that two parameters must be included with every call: query, which represents the keywords you are searching on, and Key, which is the Technorati API key. The Technorati key is generated for each individual user of the service, to prevent abuse, and you are limited to 500 API calls a day. This limit prevents someone from opening up their own site and using the Technorati's APIs as a back end, which would be like opening a restaurant and ordering takeout from another restaurant for your customers. And if you think back to when you were creating your own mashups, some blocks required keys to use for exactly the same reason.

To get your key, click the API Key tab in the Technorati Development Center. Follow the instructions until you are presented with your API key (see Figure 9-6). Make note of your API key; you will need it as we start building your block in VWD.

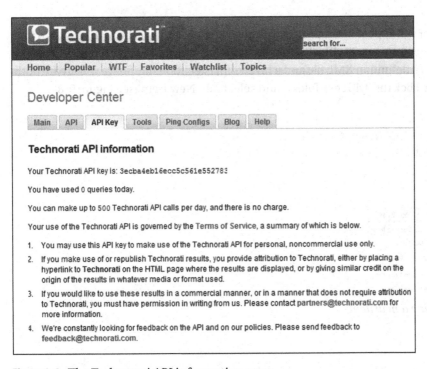

Figure 9-6. *The Technorati API information page*

Developing Your Block in Visual Web Developer

Now that we have decided on a service to use and a particular operation to start our block with, we can return to the Block SDK and VWD. Start VWD, and return to the project that we created for the Block SDK in Chapter 8. We want to add a folder to the SDK to hold the development files we'll be creating. You can do this by going to the VWD Solution Explorer, right-clicking the project icon (see Figure 9-7), and selecting New Folder.

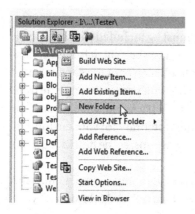

Figure 9-7. *Right-click the project, and select New Folder to add a folder to the SDK.*

A new folder will appear in the project list called NewFolder. It will be highlighted so that you can rename it, so type **MyBlocks**. Remember what you learned in Chapter 7—blocks are made up of a definition XML file and a JavaScript execution file. So we will create both of them. Right-click the MyBlocks folder, and select Add New Item (see Figure 9-8).

Figure 9-8. *Adding a new item*

We will be creating the JavaScript file first, so select JScript File from the Add New Item dialog box (see Figure 9-9).

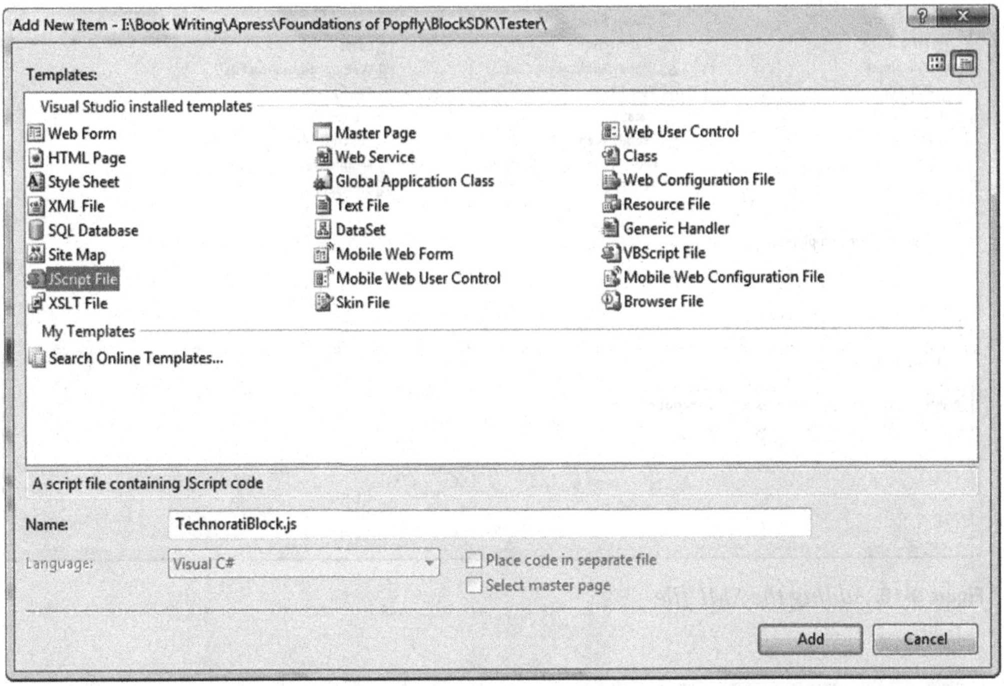

Figure 9-9. *Adding the JavaScript file*

Type **TechnoratiBlock.js** into the name field and then click the Add button. A file named TechnoratiBlock.js will appear in the MyBlocks folder.

Now, we need to create the XML definition file. Right-click and select Add New Item again. When the Add New Item dialog box appears, select XML File as the file we will be creating, type **TechnoratiDefinition.xml** in the Name field, and click the Add button (see Figure 9-10).

Your MyBlocks folder should have both the TechnoratiBlock.js and TechnoratiBlockDescription.xml files in it now (see Figure 9-11).

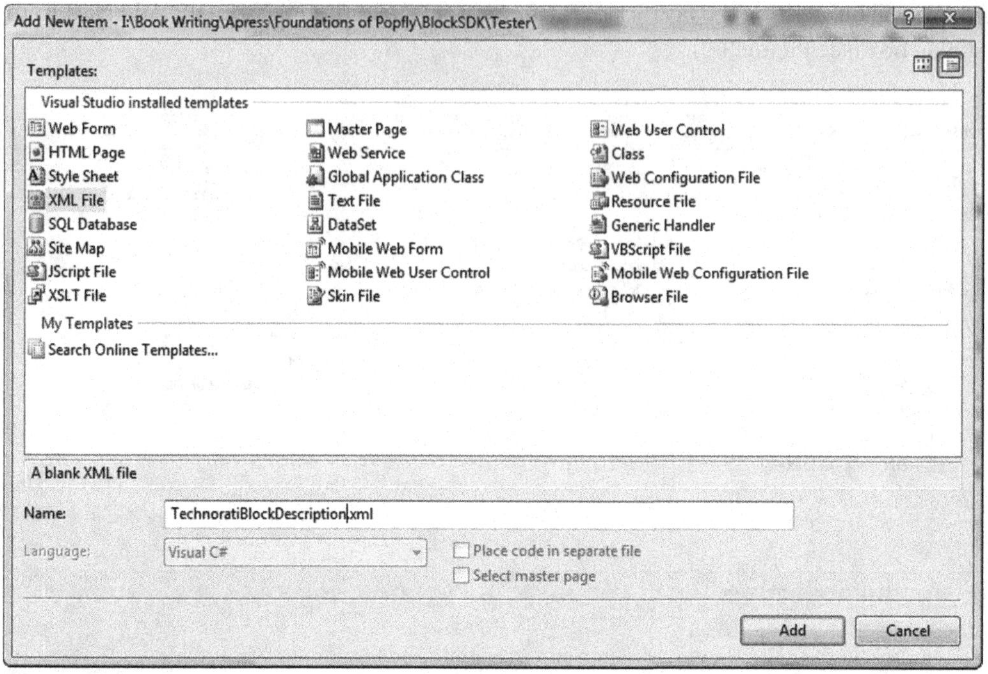

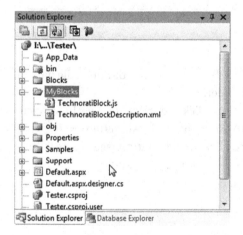

Figure 9-10. *Adding the XML file*

Figure 9-11. *The MyBlocks folder with your two new files in it*

We will work on the definition XML file after we have gotten some code working. Double-click the `TechnoratiBlock.js` file, and enter the code shown in Listing 9-1.

Listing 9-1. *TechnoratiBlock.js*

```
componentManager.add("t", "TechnoratiClass", ➥
"/content/components/icons/logo.png",
"/content/components/icons/logo.png");



function TechnoratiClass()
{
}



TechnoratiClass.prototype.getSearchResults = function(search)
{
    var api_key = "?key=";
    var callingAPI = "http://api.technorati.com/search";

    var apiKey = "[YOUR API KEY]"; //"{{Key:key;http://api.technorati.com/}}";

    var reqUrl = callingAPI;

    reqUrl += api_key + apiKey;
    reqUrl += "&query=" + search;  // can be link or weblog

    reqUrl += "&format=rss";    // set the returning xml to rss format

    var resultXML = environment.getXml(reqUrl, "technorati");

    var resultArray  = new Array();

    if(resultXML.getElementsByTagName("channel").length >= 1)
    {
        var errorCheck resultXML.getElementsByTagName("channel")[0].
getElementsByTagName("description")[0].text;
        errorLength = errorCheck.indexOf('Error');

        if(!resultXML)
        {
            throw "Sorry, the Technorati block➥
encountered a problem which it could not solve.";
        }
        if(errorLength != -1)
        {
```

```
try
{
    throw resultXML.getElementsByTagName("channel")[0].
getElementsByTagName("description")[0].text;
}
catch(ex)
{
    throw "Sorry, the Technorati block encountered a problem which
it could not solve.";
}
}
else
{
    var itemNodeList = resultXML.getElementsByTagName('item');
    var resultNodeCount = itemNodeList.length;
    var resultArray  = new Array(resultNodeCount);

    if(!resultNodeCount || resultNodeCount < 1)
    {
        throw "Sorry, it seems that the Techorati search results ➥
does not contain any items.";
    }

    for(var i = 0; i < resultNodeCount; i++)
    {
        var itemNode = itemNodeList[i];
        if(itemNode)
        {
            var title =        itemNode➥
.getElementsByTagName("title").length >= 1 ?➥
itemNode.getElementsByTagName("title")[0].text : "";
            var source =        itemNode➥
.getElementsByTagName("source").length>= 1 ?
        itemNode.getElementsByTagName("source")[0].text : "";
            var sourceLink =     ➥
itemNode.getElementsByTagName("source").length>= 1 ?
        itemNode.getElementsByTagName("source")[0].getAttribute("url") : "";
            var link =➥
itemNode.getElementsByTagName("link").length >= 1 ?
 itemNode.getElementsByTagName("link")[0].text : "";
            var description =➥
itemNode.getElementsByTagName("description").length >= 1 ?➥
```

```
itemNode.getElementsByTagName("description")[0].text : "";
                    var author =        itemNode➡
.getElementsByTagName("author").length >= 1 ?
itemNode.getElementsByTagName("author")[0].text : "";
                    var tags =          itemNode➡
.getElementsByTagName("tags").length >= 1 ?
itemNode.getElementsByTagName("tags")[0].text : "";
                    var comments =➡
itemNode.getElementsByTagName("comments").length >= 1 ?
      itemNode.getElementsByTagName("comments")[0].text : "";
                    var commentRss =    itemNode➡
.getElementsByTagName("wfw:commentRss");

                 if(commentRss.length == 0)
                    commentRss = itemNode➡
.getElementsByTagName("commentRss");

                 if(commentRss && commentRss.length > 0)
                    commentRss = commentRss[0].text;

                 var pubDate =        itemNode➡
.getElementsByTagName("pubDate").length >= 1 ?
   itemNode.getElementsByTagName("pubDate")[0].text : "";
                 var mediaLink =    itemNode➡
.getElementsByTagName("enclosure").length>= 1 ?
     itemNode.getElementsByTagName("enclosure")[0].getAttribute("url") : "";
                 var mediaType =     itemNode➡
.getElementsByTagName("enclosure").length>= 1 ?
     itemNode.getElementsByTagName("enclosure")[0].getAttribute("type") : "";

                 var lat =  itemNode➡
.getElementsByTagName("geo:lat");
                 var lon = itemNode➡
.getElementsByTagName("geo:long");

                 if(lat && lat.length == 0)
                    lat = itemNode.getElementsByTagName("lat");

                 if(lat && lat.length > 0)
                    lat = lat[0].text;
```

```
                        if(lon && lon.length == 0)
                            lon = itemNode.getElementsByTagName("long");

                        if(lon && lon.length > 0)
                            lon = lon[0].text;

                        resultArray[i] = new RSSItem(title, link, description,➥
source, sourceLink,  author,
    tags, comments, commentRss, pubDate, mediaLink, mediaType, lat, lon);
                    }
                }

            return resultArray;
            }
        }
        else
        {


            return resultArray;
        }
    }


    function RSSItem(title, link, description, source,➥
sourceLink, author, tags, comments,
 commentRss, pubDate, mediaLink, mediaType, lat, lon)
    {
        this.title = title;
        this.link = link;
        this.description = description;
        this.source= source;
        this.sourceLink= sourceLink;
        this.author = author;
        this.tags= tags;
        this.comments = comments;
        this.commentRss = commentRss;
        this.publishedDate = pubDate;
        this.mediaLink = mediaLink;
        this.mediaType = mediaType;
        this.latitude = lat;
        this.longtitude = lon;
    }
```

```
RSSItem.prototype.toString = function() {

    var html = "";

    html += "<strong>" + this.title + "</strong>";
    html += "<br /><font style='font-size: xx-small'>"➡
+ this.publishedDate +"</font>" + "\n";
    html += "<p>"+ this.description +"</p><hr/>";

    return html;
};
```

From Chapter 8, you know that the first line of code should be used to load the component into the test harness, so we can add that as the first line of our block.

```
componentManager.add("t", "TechnoratiClass",➡
"/content/components/icons/logo.png",➡
"/content/components/icons/logo.png");
```

The componentManager operation add is called with t for the variable and TechnoratiClass as the name of the JavaScript object to be created for the block. The first code of the block is an empty constructor:

```
function TechnoratiClass()
{
}
```

This JavaScript function is the first one called when the environment creates your block. You can do many things here, like initialize variables and other things the object will need later on. Since we want to keep things simple, we don't have any code in here. Remember, you must have this code, even if the function is empty, and its name must be the same as the class passed to the componentManager add operation.

First, we need to create an operation that will be used to call the Technorati APIs. We will call it getSearchResults. To create the operation in JavaScript, you use this code:

```
TechnoratiClass.prototype.getSearchResults = function(search)
```

This operation is defined with one parameter. search. It will contain the keywords entered into the block and passed into the API search function.

As you look into the code of the getSearchResults JavaScript function (see Listing 9-2), you will notice several variables created to store parts of the URL that we need to create when calling the search operation. Note that you need to insert your personal API key for [YOUR API KEY]. There is some commented code next to the apiKey variable that will be used when we define the block in XML; it is a lookup used by the Popfly environment to retrieve the API key entered by the mashup creator. For testing purposes, we are going to insert our API key directly into the code.

The rest of the code combines several string variables (apikey, callingAPI, apiKey) in the variable reqUrl to form the URL required by the search operation (i.e., http://api.technorati.com/search?key=[your_apikey]&query=[search_variable]).

Listing 9-2. *Calling the Technorati API*

```
var apikey = "?key=";
var callingAPI = "http://api.technorati.com/search";

var apiKey = "[YOUR API KEY]"; //"{{Key:key;http://api.technorati.com/}}";

var reqUrl = callingAPI;

reqUrl += apikey + apiKey;
reqUrl += "&query=" + search;   // can be link or weblog

reqUrl += "&format=rss";    // set the returning xml to rss format

var resultXML = environment.getXml(reqUrl, "technorati");
```

We are using an optional parameter called format that indicates that we would like to receive the results of the search in RSS format. RSS format is not only common on the Internet but in many blocks within Popfly. This choice will give us some flexibility, because more blocks that can interact with our block.

The Popfly helper object environment's getXml function is called with built reqUrl variable being passed to it. The results returned are XML in RSS format and are assigned to a variable called resultXML. The remaining code of the block should look very familiar. Most of the code was grabbed directly from the RSS block in Chapter 7. This is one of the important principles you need to learn when creating your blocks: reusing code will speed your development, because that code works and has been tested. Nothing is wrong with creating your own code from scratch, but you can save a lot of headaches by leveraging the work of others.

The RSS XML is parsed, and an array of RSSItem objects is created and returned as the result of the function. Now, any block that consumes an object of type RSSItem can consume the results of our Technorati block.

Testing Your Block

Now that we have the block code ready, it's time to test the code to make sure it works. To test it, we need to get it working in the SDK's test harness. In Chapter 8, we got the test harness up and running, and you learned how it works. You know that, for code to be loaded into the test harness, it has to be in the Blocks folder. And now that we have completed writing the code, we can move the TechnoratiBlock.js file into the Blocks folder (see Figure 9-12).

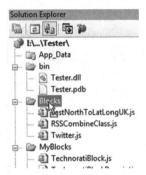

Figure 9-12. *Moving the TechnoratiBlock.js*

Remember that the lines at the top of the code will load the block class using the componentManager add operation.

Select Debug ➤ Start Debugging. A browser window will open with the test harness running. You should see "Loaded Block:TechnoratiClass." displayed at the bottom of the harness window.

Delete any code that is in the test harness code text box, and type the following (see Figure 9-13):

```
t= new TechnoratiClass()
t.getSearchResults("Silverlight")
```

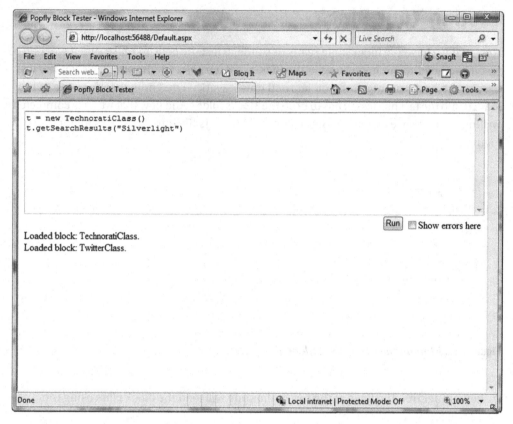

Figure 9-13. *Testing TechnoratiClass*

Click the Run button to see the results shown in Figure 9-14. After the call is made to the search operation of the Technorati API, the results are stored in an array of RSSItems. In Chapter 8, you also learned that the RSSItem has an operation called toString that is used to express the contents of the RSSItem as HTML. So after the XML from the search operation is returned, it is parsed into an array of RSSItems. Each one of the RSSItem's toString functions is called by the test harness to display the results in HTML.

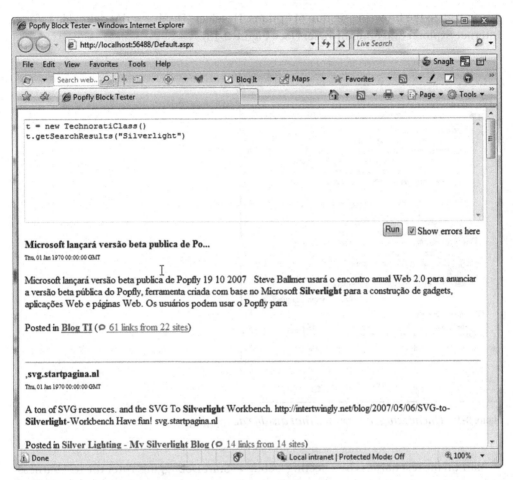

Figure 9-14. *Results of calling getSearchResults*

Debugging Your Code with Visual Web Developer

You just ran your code in the test harness successfully the first time! Unfortunately, that is not likely to happen all the time. Nobody is perfect, so you need to know how to fix problems with your code. Fortunately, VWD has powerful debugging capabilities that you can use.

The test harness doesn't have this capability. Errors can be displayed, but they won't help you much. Apparently, the Popfly team didn't spend a lot of time building a robust error reporting functionality. Errors like "Object unidentified" or "Object not found" don't help you track down where the problem is. To display errors in the test harness anyway, check the "Show errors here" check box.

The first thing you need to do to debug your code using VWD is to enable debugging in Internet Explorer. You can do that by selecting Tools ➤ Internet Options. Click the Advanced tab, and go to the Browsing section of options. Deselect "Disable script debugging" for Internet Explorer and other browsers (see Figure 9-15).

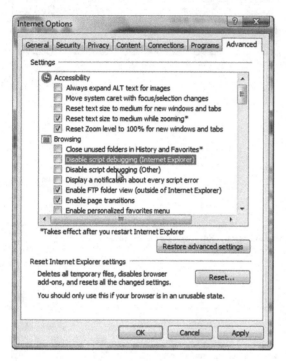

Figure 9-15. *Unchecking the options that disable debugging*

Start up the test harness by selecting Debug ➤ Start Debugging. After the test harness appears in Internet Explorer, go into VWD, and open the Script Explorer by selecting Debug ➤ Windows ➤ Script Explorer (see Figure 9-16).

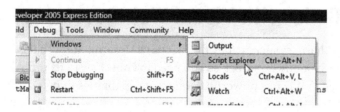

Figure 9-16. *Opening the Script Explorer*

The Script Explorer should open, and you can see all of the JavaScript files that can be debugged (see Figure 9-17).

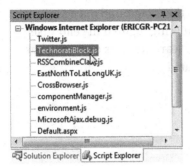

Figure 9-17. *Script Explorer*

Now that we are ready to debug, we are going to set a break point. A break point is like a bookmark that stops the execution of code at the point where you place it. In this way, you can inspect the code around the breakpoint to look for errors. It's better to show than explain, so let's create a breakpoint.

Open the `TechnoratiBlock.js` file by double-clicking it in the Script Explorer. Right-click the line `var resultXML = environment.getXml(reqUrl, "technorati");`.

The menu shown in Figure 9-18 will appear. Select Breakpoint ➤ Insert Breakpoint. The line should be highlighted in red.

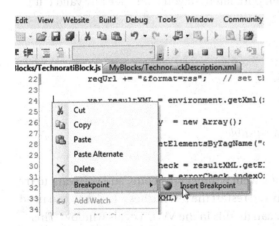

Figure 9-18. *Setting a breakpoint*

Now that we have a breakpoint set, let's debug the code by going back to the test harness running in Internet Explorer and again typing

```
t= new TechnoratiClass()
t.getSearchResults("Silverlight")
```

Click the Run button. VWD will automatically come to the foreground once the break-point is hit. This time, code on the line of the breakpoint is highlighted in yellow (see Figure 9-19): all of the code above the highlight in the getSearchResults operation has been executed; all of the code below it has yet to be executed.

```
19      requrl += api_key + apikey;
20      reqUrl += "&query=" + search;  // can be link or weblog
21
22      reqUrl += "&format=rss";   // set the returning xml to rss
23
24      var resultXML = environment.getXml(reqUrl, "technorati");
25
26      var resultArray  = new Array();
27
28      if(resultXML.getElementsByTagName("channel").length >= 1)
29      {
```

Figure 9-19. *The breakpoint is hit.*

If that is the case, the reqUrl variable should be populated with the query for the search function. You can verify that by holding the mouse over the variable, as shown in Figure 9-20. You should see the URL built by the code preceding it (e.g., http://api.technorati.com/search?key={YOURAPIKEY}&query=Silverlight&format=rss).

You can do this for any of the variables in the code. Remember, though, that if the variable is below the breakpoint line, it has not been populated, so you won't see any valid data.

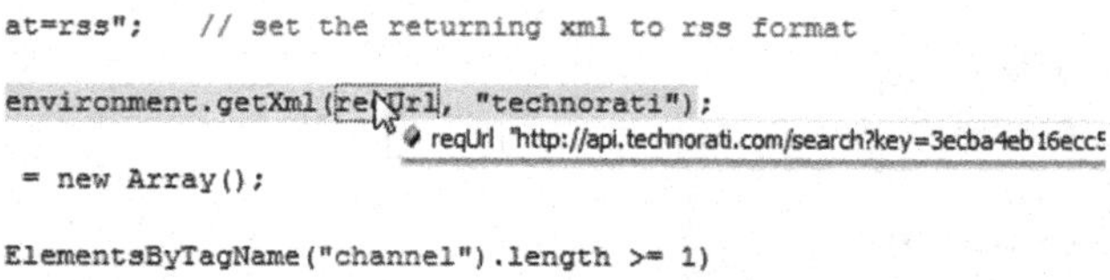

```
at=rss";   // set the returning xml to rss format

environment.getXml(reqUrl, "technorati");
                    ⦿ reqUrl "http://api.technorati.com/search?key=3ecba4eb16ecc5

 = new Array();

ElementsByTagName("channel").length >= 1)
```

Figure 9-20. *Breakpoint hit and examining a variable*

OK, so you are working on why something went wrong in the code, and you want to try something different without having to stop and restart the test harness. Let's say you need to change a variable to another value. You can do this in the VWD Locals window. This window shows all of the variables that are defined in your JavaScript code. You can inspect the values and even change the values if the code is paused in a breakpoint. It should already be showing at the bottom to the VWD window. But you can show it by selecting Debug ➤ Windows ➤ Locals (see Figure 9-21). The Locals window has a list of all of the objects (some created by you, others created by other code) that you can inspect and change. You can see the reqUrl variable in the list also.

Locals			▼ ⨥ ×
Name	Value	Type	▲
🔷 search	"Silverlight"	String	
🔷 api_key	"?key="	String	
🔷 callingAPI	"http://api.technorati.com/search"	String	E
🔷 apiKey	"3ecba4eb16ecc5c561e5527830677a86"	String	
🔷 reqUrl	"http://api.technrati.com/search?key=3ecba4eb16ecc5c561e5527830677a86&query	String	
🔷 resultXML	undefined	User-defi	
🔷 resultArray	undefined	User-defi	
🔷 errorCheck	undefined	User-defi	
🔷 ex	undefined	User-defi	
🔷 itemNodeList	undefined	User-defi	
🔷 resultNodeCount	undefined	User-defi	
🔷 i	undefined	User-defi	▾
🗗 Locals 🗗 Watch			

Figure 9-21. *The Locals window*

Expand the Value cell to show more of the data. Double-click the reqUrl, and change
the value of the query from Silverlight to Popfly (see Figure 9-22).

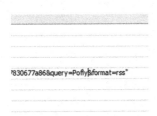

?830677a86&query=Pofly&format=rss"

Figure 9-22. *The Locals window*

What we have just done is change the call to the search operation as if we typed it in the
test harness. To see the results of the change, select Debug ➤ Continue. The results displayed
in the test harness should reflect a search on "Popfly", not "Silverlight". This is the power
of debugging—the ability to make minor changes to see the impact on your code.

VWD is a great tool for debugging your block JavaScript code. I would advise reading
more about debugging in the VWD documentation to discover some of the other features
available to you.

Creating Your Block Definition with Visual Web Developer

A block's definition used by the PRE is an XML file. XML files can be edited in any text
editor, such as Notepad. However, Notepad doesn't help you with the trickier parts of
writing XML documents. In particular, it doesn't validate the XML document to prevent

errors. VWD has a built-in editor that provides a rich environment to create error-free XML documents.

Stop debugging, and return to VWD and the Solution Explorer. Double-click the TechnoratiBlockDefinition.xml file to open it in the VWD editor. To take advantage of the features in VWD's editor, we need to attach the Popfly Block Definition XML schema file, called BlockSchema.xsd, to the document; you can find it in the root folder of the SDK ("XSD" means XML schema definition). VWD uses these schema files to validate and help you create XML documents. XML schemas are a standard way to define the structure of an XML document.

To attach the schema file to the document, go to the Properties window (see Figure 9-23).

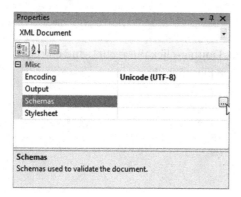

Figure 9-23. *The Properties window*

Click the Schemas cell to show the ellipsis button to the right of the cell. Click that button to show the XSD Schemas dialog box (see Figure 9-24), which lists schemas registered with VWD.

The BlockSchema.xsd file is not located in the list, so we have to add it. Click the Add button to open a file dialog box. Locate the directory with the schema file (it should be in the root directory of the SDK you installed). After you select it, you should see it in the list. Make sure to put a check mark in the box next to it when it appears (see Figure 9-25).

Close all the dialog boxes, and return to the editor. Type < in the editor to see the "block" element appear in the drop-down list (see Figure 9-26). This drop-down is a feature of VWD called Intellisense. It takes your input and gives you valid selections based on the schema attached to the XML file.

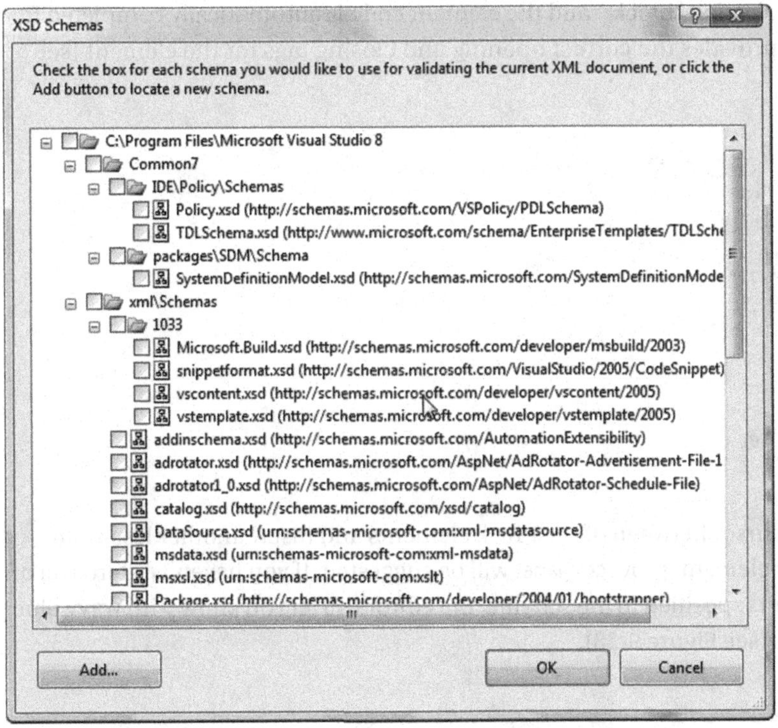

XSD Schemas

Check the box for each schema you would like to use for validating the current XML document, or click the Add button to locate a new schema.

- ☐ 📁 C:\Program Files\Microsoft Visual Studio 8
  - ☐ 📁 Common7
    - ☐ 📁 IDE\Policy\Schemas
      - ☐ 🗊 Policy.xsd (http://schemas.microsoft.com/VSPolicy/PDLSchema)
      - ☐ 🗊 TDLSchema.xsd (http://www.microsoft.com/schema/EnterpriseTemplates/TDLSche
    - ☐ 📁 packages\SDM\Schema
      - ☐ 🗊 SystemDefinitionModel.xsd (http://schemas.microsoft.com/SystemDefinitionMode
  - ☐ 📁 xml\Schemas
    - ☐ 📁 1033
      - ☐ 🗊 Microsoft.Build.xsd (http://schemas.microsoft.com/developer/msbuild/2003)
      - ☐ 🗊 snippetformat.xsd (http://schemas.microsoft.com/VisualStudio/2005/CodeSnippet)
      - ☐ 🗊 vscontent.xsd (http://schemas.microsoft.com/developer/vscontent/2005)
      - ☐ 🗊 vstemplate.xsd (http://schemas.microsoft.com/developer/vstemplate/2005)
    - ☐ 🗊 addinschema.xsd (http://schemas.microsoft.com/AutomationExtensibility)
    - ☐ 🗊 adrotator.xsd (http://schemas.microsoft.com/AspNet/AdRotator-Advertisement-File-1
    - ☐ 🗊 adrotator1_0.xsd (http://schemas.microsoft.com/AspNet/AdRotator-Schedule-File)
    - ☐ 🗊 catalog.xsd (http://schemas.microsoft.com/xsd/catalog)
    - ☐ 🗊 DataSource.xsd (urn:schemas-microsoft-com:xml-msdatasource)
    - ☐ 🗊 msdata.xsd (urn:schemas-microsoft-com:xml-msdata)
    - ☐ 🗊 msxsl.xsd (urn:schemas-microsoft-com:xslt)
    - ☐ 🗊 Package.xsd (http://schemas.microsoft.com/developer/2004/01/bootstrapper)

[Add...]   [OK]   [Cancel]

Figure 9-24. *The Properties window*

- ☐ 🗊 xsdschema.xsd (http://www.w3.org/2001/XMLScher
- ☐ 🗊 xslt.xsd (http://www.w3.org/1999/XSL/Transform)
- ☑ 📁 I:\Book Writing\Apress\Foundations of Popfly\BlockSDK
  - ☑ 🗊 BlockSchema.xsd

Figure 9-25. *The BlockSchema is selected.*

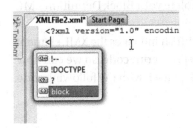

Figure 9-26. *Intellisense in action*

Press Tab after selecting "block," and the element code is automatically completed for you. Notice that it provides the correct opening and closing tags for the element (see Figure 9-27).

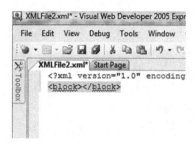

Figure 9-27. *Intellisense*

If you place the cursor between of the block elements and insert another less-than symbol (<), another element, providerName, will be suggested. If you haven't entered all of the required elements specified in the schema, the editor will let you know with wavy blue lines under the tags (see Figure 9-28).

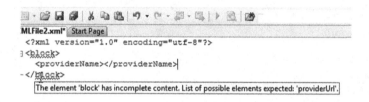

Figure 9-28. *XML Schema validation*

Now that you've seen how the editor can help you complete your Block Definition XML file, you're ready to look at the complete definition in Listing 9-3.

Notice the area under keys, which sets up things for the PRE. It indicates the XML element that will be used for storing and retrieving the key in your JavaScript code, so we can now uncomment the section of code that uses the API key and replace it with the following code:

```
var apiKey = "{{Key:key;http://api.technorati.com/}}";
```

The string assigned to the apiKey variable indicates that it is to look up the value of the API key in the key attribute defined in the keys section of the definition file.

Listing 9-3. *Technorati Block Definition XML File*

```xml
<?xml version="1.0" encoding="utf-8" ?>
<block class="TechnoratiClass">
  <providerName>Technorati</providerName>
  <providerUrl>http://www.technorati.com/</providerUrl>
  <providerLogoUrl>/content/components/icons/block.png</providerLogoUrl>
  <blockIconUrl>/content/components/icons/block.png</blockIconUrl>
  <keys>
    <description/>
    <signUpUrl>http://technorati.com/developers/apikey.html</signUpUrl>
    <key id="key" whenRequired="save">
      <name>API Key</name>
      <notes/>
    </key>
  </keys>
  <operations>
    <operation name="getSearchResults" callMode="auto">
      <description>Blog posts featuring a given ➡
                                keyword or phrase(Items Only) Returned in RSS
format.</description>
      <inputs>
        <input name="query" required="true" type="string">
          <description>Set this to the words you are searching for.</description>
          <defaultValue>Popfly</defaultValue>
          <constraints/>
        </input>
      </inputs>
      <outputs>
        <output isArray="true" type="custom" object="RSSItem"/>
      </outputs>
    </operation>
  </operations>
  <objects>
    <object name="RSSItem">
      <field name="title" type="title" isArray="false"/>
      <field name="link" type="url" isArray="false"/>
      <field name="description" type="description" isArray="false"/>
      <field name="source" type="string" isArray="false"/>
      <field name="sourceLink" type="url" isArray="false"/>
      <field name="author" type="name" isArray="false"/>
      <field name="tags" type="string" isArray="false"/>
      <field name="comments" type="string" isArray="false"/>
```

```
            <field name="commentRss" type="string" isArray="false"/>
            <field name="publishedDate" type="date" isArray="false"/>
            <field name="mediaLink" type="url" isArray="false"/>
            <field name="mediaType" type="string" isArray="false"/>
            <field name="latitude" type="latitude" isArray="false"/>
            <field name="longtitude" type="longitude" isArray="false"/>
        </object>
    </objects>
</block>
```

Now that we have written the code and defined the block in a block definition file, we are ready to return to Popfly to test the code in a mashup. It will also give us an opportunity to explore block development using Popfly's block creator.

Summary

In this chapter, you have learned how to use the rich functionality within Microsoft's Visual Web Developer (VWD) to create blocks using the Popfly Block SDK. You've learned how to edit a block's JavaScript file and block definition files in its editor. You've also learned about VWD's debugging capabilities and how to use the Block SDK schema files to help write and validate block definition files.

In the next chapter, we'll return to the Popfly web site and explore the Popfly block creation area.

■ ■ ■

CHAPTER 10

Using the Popfly Block Creator

In Chapter 9, you learned about how to use Visual Web Developer (VWD) to create a block using the Popfly SDK without using the Popfly environment. To use your new block, you have to get it into the Popfly environment, which you can accomplish using the Block Creator. In this chapter, we will explore how to use the Block Creator to create, share, and copy blocks created by Microsoft's and other block creators.

The Block Creator

The Popfly Block Creator can be opened by selecting Create Stuff ➤ Block from the main menu. The Block Creator will open an unsaved block (see Figure 10-1).

The Block Creator has two editing views: Block Description (which defines the operations and properties of the block) and Block Code (which executes the functionality of the block). Toggle between by clicking the tabs. When a block is first created, you see XML and JavaScript comments prompting you to place your description and code into the respective editors. To the left of the editors is the familiar Blocks window. If you recall, this window contains the categorized list of blocks that are available to use in Popfly.

You can easily find blocks by typing keywords into the search box at the top of the window. In Chapter 7, we examined the code of the RSS block. To find that block here, type **RSS** into the search box. You should see the results in the Blocks window (see Figure 10-2).

Figure 10-1. *The initial page of the Popfly Block Creator*

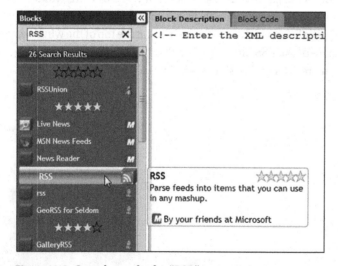

Figure 10-2. *Search results for "RSS"*

Hover the mouse over the RSS block to see additional information, including the block's description and author. In this case, the author is Microsoft. If we were in the mashup creator, double-clicking or dragging and dropping the RSS block would create a new block. In the Block Creator, double-clicking the RSS block copies, or rips, the code from the RSS block into both editors. Double-click the RSS block; your Block Creator will show the code ripped from the RSS block, as in Figure 10-3.

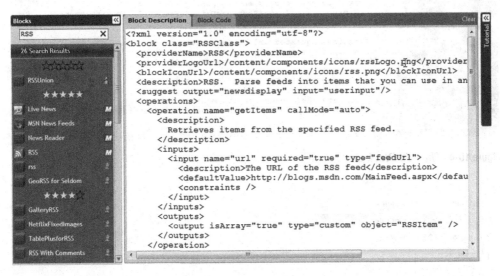

Figure 10-3. *The RSS Block Description view*

Ripping code using the Block Creator is how I got the code for the RSS block for Chapter 7, and it's a great way to get started on your own block and learn by examining code from other authors. In this case, learning from the Popfly team at Microsoft can shorten your development time and reduce your learning curve. Click the Block Code tab to see the source code (see Figure 10-4)

Again, the RSS block code is the same RSS code we examined in Chapter 7. Both the Block Code and Block Description editors are very basic and don't compare to the robust environment of VWD.

However, the Block Code editor does have some of the functionality you would expect from an advanced environment, such as a limited code-completion functionality that helps you complete your code and use Popfly's built-in helper objects and other utility functions.

Place the cursor in a location in the editor, and begin typing a letter. A drop-down menu should appear below where you are typing (see Figure 10-5).

```
Blocks                    «   Block Description | Block Code                                    Clear  «
RSS                       ×       function RSSClass()          I
26 Search Results                 {
        ☆☆☆☆☆               }

RSSUnion                          // Pass the requested url to base class function and get the forma
        ★★★★★               RSSClass.prototype.getFeed = function (url) {
Live News            M              // Retrieves information about the specified RSS feed.
MSN News Feeds       M              //
News Reader          M              // url (required): The URL of the RSS feed.
RSS                  M                  this.__checkValidation(url);
rss                                     var returnResponse = environment.getXml(url);
GeoRSS for Seldom                       return this.__formatResponseDataRSSFeed(url, returnResponse);
        ★★★★☆               };

GalleryRSS                        // Pass the requested url to base class function and get the forma
NetflixFixedImages                RSSClass.prototype.getItems = function (url){
TablePlusforRSS                     // Retrieves items from the specified RSS feed.
RSS With Comments                   //
                                    // url (required): The URL of the RSS feed.
                                        this.__checkValidation(url);
                                        var returnResponse = environment.getXml(url);
                                        return this.__formatResponseDataRSSItem(returnResponse);
                                  };
```

Figure 10-4. *The RSS Block Code view*

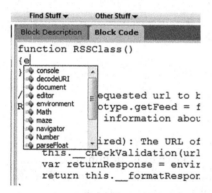

Figure 10-5. *The Block Editor code-completion functionality*

You can use the scroll bar to see all of the available objects and functions. Select the "environment" object from the list and press Tab. The word "environment" should be added to the editor. Type a period after the word "environment," and another drop-down menu will appear showing the available properties and operations of the Popfly environment object (see Figure 10-6). You should remember the important getXml function, which allows you to retrieve XML data from web service, from our code in Chapters 7, 8, and 9. Select "getXml" to insert it into the editor.

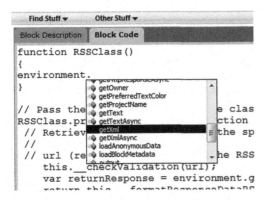

Figure 10-6. *Selecting the getXml operation*

After the operation has been inserted, you can gain further information about it, like the parameters that it requires, by typing the opening parenthesis (see Figure 10-7). In this case, the getXml operation is shown to have four parameters.

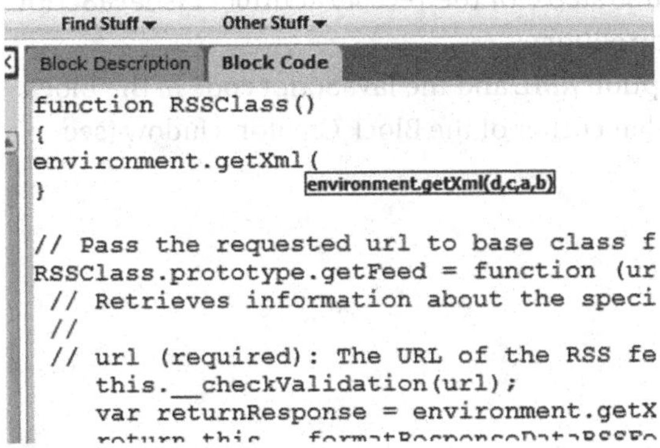

Figure 10-7. *Showing operation information*

Adding Your Block to Popfly

Now that you have seen what the Block Creator has to offer in the way of editing the code for your block, let's add the block we've been working on.

In the Block Creator, create a new blank block by Selecting Create Stuff➤ Block. Open VWD to the project that contains the Technorati block we created in Chapter 9 (see Figure 10-8).

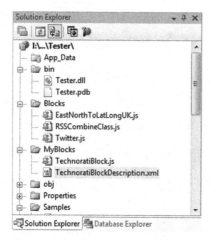

Figure 10-8. *Showing operation information*

Open the MyBlocks folder, and double-click the TechnoratiBlockDescription.xml file to open it in the editor. Select all the XML, and copy and paste it into the Block Description editor in the Block Creator. Repeat the same steps for the TechnoratiBlock.js JavaScript code, but paste the code in the Block Code editor.

Now, you should have both the description XML and the JavaScript code in the Block Creator. Click the Save button at the top-left corner of the Block Creator window (see Figure 10-9).

Figure 10-9. *Saving the block*

Once you click the button, the Save As dialog box appears (see Figure 10-10). Enter **MyTechnoratiBlock** as the name project. You can also add a description for other people to see and a tag that will be used to help others search for your block.

Click the Accept and Save button to save your block. Once you return to the Block Creator, you should be able to see your block under the My Blocks section of the Block window (you might have to refresh your browser); see Figure 10-11.

Now that your block has been added to the Popfly environment, you are ready to use it in your mashups.

If you are not in the Block Creator, you can find your block in your Projects list by selecting My Stuff ➤ Projects from the main menu. When the Projects list appears, your block will be at the top of the list (see Figure 10-12).

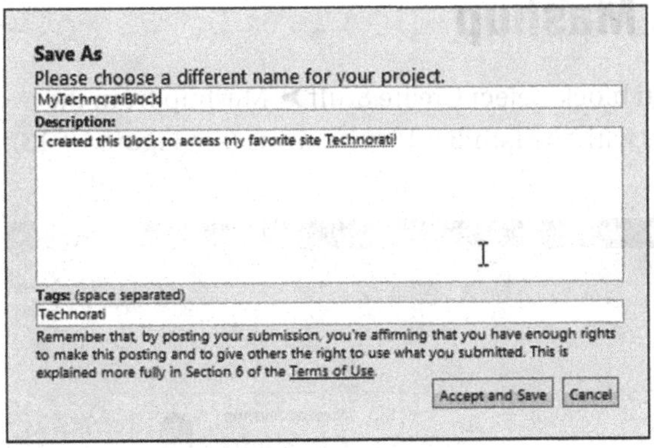

Save As
Please choose a different name for your project.
MyTechnoratiBlock
Description:
I created this block to access my favorite site Technorati!
Tags: (space separated)
Technorati
Remember that, by posting your submission, you're affirming that you have enough rights to make this posting and to give others the right to use what you submitted. This is explained more fully in Section 6 of the Terms of Use.
Accept and Save
Cancel

Figure 10-10. *The Save As dialog box*

Tools
Everything Else
My Blocks
MyTechnoratiBlock
MyTechnoratiBlock
I created this block to access my favorite site Technorati!
By you! (not shared)

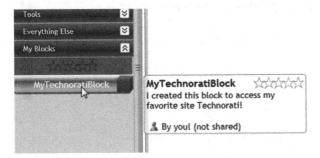

Figure 10-11. *Your block appears under My Blocks.*

My Stuff
Find Stuff
Other Stuff
Projects
MyTechnoratiBlock
Last Edited: Friday, November 02, 2007 1:50:47 PM
Private
Project Details
Edit
Delete
Share
My Photo Mashup
This has 1 rating:

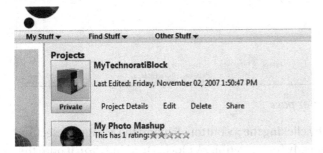

Figure 10-12. *Your block in the Projects list*

From the Projects list, you can click Project Details, Delete, or Edit to modify your project in the Block Creator. Sharing your block is easy, too: click the Share link to publish it to the Popfly community.

Using Your Block in a Mashup

To create a mashup with the Technorati block, select Create Stuff ➤ Mashup from the main menu. The mashup creator opens with the familiar blank canvas (see Figure 10-13).

Figure 10-13. *The blank mashup creator page*

Minimize the Tutorial window by clicking the >> button. Expand the My Blocks section of the Blocks window, and locate the MyTechnoratiBlock block. Drag and drop it onto the canvas (see Figure 10-14). Place the mouse over the block to show the block's help tip. The operation we wrote, "getSearchResults," is the default and only operation displayed, with its sole parameter "query" and the default value of "Popfly."

Double-click the block to display the simple view of the operation (see Figure 10-15), which shows the information we defined in the block description. There is no drop-down menu of operations, because our block has only one. The description of the operation, also retrieved from our block definition, is displayed before the operation name. The parameters list displays the "query" variable, and the default value "Popfly" has been entered in the textbox.

Figure 10-14. *The MyTechnoratiBlock*

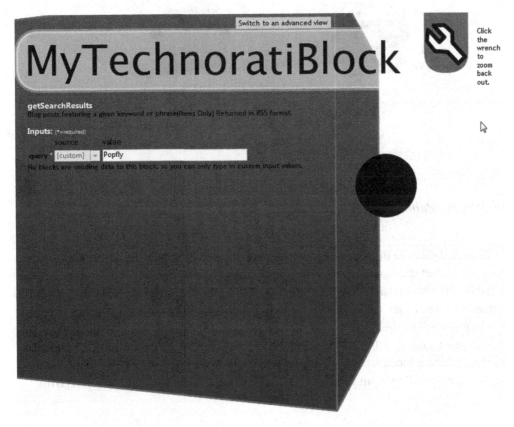

Figure 10-15. *Operation details*

Our block is not very useful by itself; it needs something to display the results from a search. We made the design decision in Chapter 9 to use the RSS XML format for retrieving data from the Technorati service and the RSSItem object as the type that will represent that data in Popfly. We did so because RSS is a common format used to transmit data from services, and the RSSItem object is a common type used to pass that data in Popfly blocks.

The News Reader block can receive the RSSItem type as an input, so it's the best object to use for our block.

Find the News Reader block in the Block window, and drag and drop it onto the mashup creator canvas (see Figure 10-16).

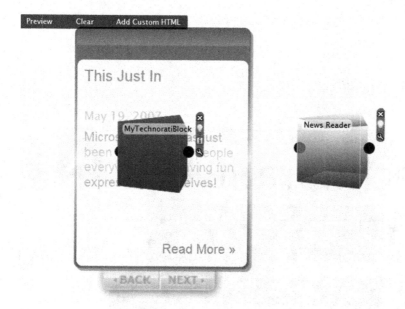

Figure 10-16. *Adding the News Reader block*

Now that we have the News Reader block and its display appearing in the background, we can connect the blocks together by joining the right side of MyTechnoratiBlock to the left side of the News Reader block (see Figure 10-17). The RSSItem array from our operation getSearchItems is passed to the News Reader block once we connect the blocks together.

Double-clicking the News Reader block displays its operation, "addNewsItem", and its inputs (see Figure 10-18). The source for all inputs is our MyTechnoratiBlock, and since the News Reader block accepts RSSItem types, the field values are recognized and matched to the corresponding input fields of "headline", "date", "content", and "fullStoryUrl".

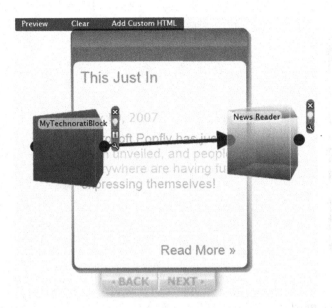

Figure 10-17. *Connecting the blocks*

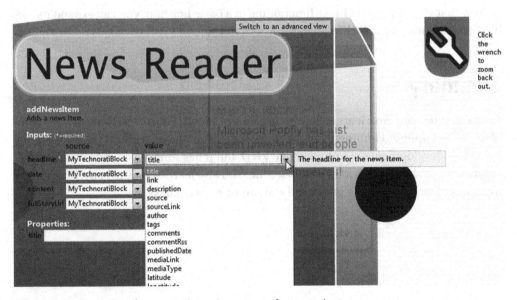

Figure 10-18. *News Reader operations, inputs, and properties*

Type **Technorati Search** into the "title" field, and since the default search value is Popfly in MyTechnoratiBlock, you can click the Preview link to display the Technorati search results using the News Reader block (see Figure 10-19).

Figure 10-19. *The Technorati Search mashup*

Now that you've got your block functioning in a basic mashup, you can expand its use by adding a User Input block to change the search values.

Summary

In this chapter, you have learned how to use Popfly's Block Creator to create or add your block to the Popfly environment for use in mashups. The Block Creator is not as rich as an integrated development environment like VWD, but it has some basic code completion functionality to help you write your block code. You also learned how to copy, or rip, code from other blocks to learn or get a head start on your own blocks

Index

You Need the Companion eBook